SALSAS
SAUCES, MARINADES & MORE

SALSAS
SAUCES, MARINADES & MORE

EXTRAORDINARY MEALS FROM
ORDINARY INGREDIENTS

Kathleen Hansel & Audrey Jenkins

CLEAR LIGHT PUBLISHERS
SANTA FE, NEW MEXICO

© 1999 Kathleen Hansel and Audrey Jenkins
Clear Light Publishers, 823 Don Diego, Santa Fe, NM 87505
WEB: www.clearlightbooks.com

First Edition
10 9 8 7 6 5 4 3 2

Library of Congress Cataloging-in-Publication Data
Hansel, Kathleen,
    Salsas, sauces, marinades and more : extraordinary meals from ordinary ingredients / Kathleen Hansel and Audrey Jenkins.
        p.   cm.
    Includes index.
    ISBN 1–57416–038–9
    1. Sauces. 2. Cookery. I. Jenkins, Audrey. II. title.
TX819.A1H36   1999
641.8'14—dc21   99-37552
                                                        CIP

Cover design: Marcia Keegan
Cover photograph: © 1999 Marcia Keegan
Typography and design: Carol O'Shea

Printed in U.S.A.

Contents

Sauces 29

Dressings 60

Marinades, Glazes & Rubs   85

Slaws   97

What's for Dinner?   126

Hot Off the Grill! 155

The Quick-Fix Pantry 164

Index 185

 Introduction

Are you sometimes so busy, so tired, or so downright uninspired that the idea of putting one more boring dinner on the table sends you straight to the telephone to order take-out? It happens to us all the time—but we have a solution! Actually, we have almost 200 solutions, and we've put them into this little book to help you banish the dinnertime doldrums and turn that simple supper into a zesty taste sensation.

Our goal was a collection of fast, uncomplicated, whip-up or chop-together condiments to turn an otherwise ordinary steak, chop, chicken breast, or fish fillet into a great flavor experience with a minimum of effort. We also wanted a few fresh vegetable and fruit salads we could serve as a main course, with or without meat. As in *The Red Chile Bible* (Clear Light 1998), we wanted to rely heavily on fresh vegetables, fruits, and greens for substance, and on chiles, garlic, ginger, peppercorns, horseradish, mustards, vinegars, and aromatic herbs for a flavor kick.

We got some great results! We love the old standbys you would expect to find in a good basic cookbook—such as Fresh Tomato Salsa, Carolina Barbecue Sauce, and Old-Fashioned Carrot Raisin Slaw. But we also love our new ideas for combining ingredients in unusual or interesting ways—such as Pear and Fennel Salsa, Honeydew and Jalapeño Coulis, and Spicy Snow Pea Slaw with Egg Ribbons. Most of these recipes involve no cooking at all, and can be chopped or whisked together in minutes with a good chef's knife or a food processor. Many of the recipes that do require some cooking can be put together and then refrigerated or frozen for later use.

Salsa! It's simply the Spanish word for "sauce," but Americans have adopted it with an exclamation mark. Salsa is among the simplest quick condiments to bring bright color and tantalizing (sometimes fiery) taste to the table, and we have included salsas to complement every kind of food and excite every palate. If it involves fresh chopped fruits or vegetables, aromatic herbs, something crunchy, and a tangy oil and acid marinade, we consider it salsa. Although most of our salsas include some fresh chile, many are only a distant relative of the typical table salsas we encounter in Latin restaurants. In fact, some of our cooked salsas are closer kin to your grandmother's savory relishes and chutneys.

Slaw! We think slaw should have an exclamation mark, too. The traditional savory bowl of shredded cabbage with a sweet and tangy boiled dressing probably arrived with the Dutch, whose "coleslaw" actually meant "cut salad." Today, the new American cuisine has brought slaw from the backyard barbecue to the formal dining table with marvelous panache. Top restaurants in Santa Fe, New Mexico, and across the country are creating vibrant new slaws to garnish and enhance everything from toasted sandwiches to grilled elk and lobster medallions. For us, the great appeal of slaw is that it's fresh, fresh, fresh, unadulterated natural food with great flavor. As a bonus, most slaws can be chopped together in only a few minutes by the most harried working cook who's long on creative imagination but short on time. As far as we're concerned, any fun and flavorful combination of slivered fresh fruits, vegetables, nuts, cheeses, meats, and greens qualifies as "slaw," the new American condiment.

We've included some tried-and-true and some unusual-and-new cabbage slaws, as well as a selection of savory fruit and vegetable slaws without a single shred of cabbage involved. Many of these recipes are hearty enough to serve as a main course meal, but our focus is on the zesty, zingy slaws that can turn your ho-hum Tuesday night haddock fillet into a gourmet delight.

Sauces and dressings are a world, a galaxy, a universe of marvelous concoctions for bringing velvety texture, flavor, and flair to simple foods—but lots of them are the sort of cooking project best reserved for grand entertaining or long, easy weekends. Our goal for this book was a collection of the fast and simple, and most of these sauces and dressings don't require any cooking at all. We've included lots of cold mayonnaise and sour cream dressings you can whip together in no time, a variety of wonderful vinaigrettes, some spicy pestos and sweet-hot fresh fruit sauces that take mere minutes to puree in a food processor, a selection of long-simmered chile and barbecue sauces (from all-American to Indian to Chinese) to keep on hand in refrigerator or freezer, and some velvety reduced cream sauces redolent of fresh herbs or special cheeses.

To bring it all together, we decided to review our basic routines for storing, preparing, and cooking the pasta, chicken, steaks, chops, and seafood that all these great sauces, salsas, and condiments are designed to enhance. We covered the quick-fix from the kitchen range to the barbecue grill.

Finally, we wanted to describe the well-stocked pantry that every cook who is working, traveling, parenting, or otherwise fully engaged in life outside the kitchen would love to come home to.

We had a good time putting these recipes together. We hope you'll find some simple and sensational concoctions to liven up your everyday meals and transform "just supper" into "just super"!

Salsas

Fresh Tomato Salsa

Everybody's favorite for dipping tortilla chips, this mild chile salsa is also great for dressing up tacos, eggs, steaks, grilled chicken, or broiled fish. If you want more fire, add another fresh chile to the bowl. Best served within 2 days.

1 pound ripe tomatoes, peeled, seeded, and chopped
    (about 2 cups)
2 fresh jalapeño or serrano chiles, seeded and
    minced
4 scallions, chopped (½ cup)
1 large garlic clove, minced
1 tablespoon fresh cilantro leaves, chopped
½ teaspoon dried oregano
2 tablespoons fresh lime juice
1 teaspoon apple cider vinegar

Combine ingredients and then cover and chill. Add salt and pepper to taste. *Yield: About 2½ cups.*

Orange and Tomato Salsa

Fresh oranges and tomatoes are a delicious flavor combination we enjoy all too seldom. This tangy salsa does beautiful things for grilled pork or fish, and is a refreshing appetizer salsa with cheeses and savory crackers. It should be served no more than 1 or 2 hours after you put it together.

> *2 large sweet oranges*
> *1 pound ripe tomatoes, peeled, seeded, finely*
>   *chopped and drained (2 cups)*
> *¼ small red onion, finely chopped (¼ cup)*
> *½ small jicama, finely diced (½ cup)*
> *1 fresh serrano chile, seeded and minced*
> *1 tablespoon fresh mint leaves, minced*
> *1 tablespoon fresh cilantro leaves, minced*
> *1 teaspoon fresh lime juice*
> *1 teaspoon white wine vinegar*
> *2 tablespoons olive oil*

Peel oranges with a sharp knife, cutting away all pith and membrane, and section carefully. Chop sections gently in half, and place in a sieve to drain thoroughly. Combine remaining ingredients, and then cover and chill for about an hour. Add salt and pepper to taste. When ready to serve, gently stir in the drained orange pieces. *Yield: About 2½ cups.*

Corn and Black Bean Salsa

This robust composition has a Southwest flair. We serve it with fresh baked tortilla chips, or as a garnish for baked sea bass or grilled steaks. This salsa can be served chilled or at room temperature, and keeps several days in the refrigerator.

1 cup black beans, cooked
1½ cups fresh corn kernels, cooked (or frozen
  kernels, thawed)
¼ small red onion, finely diced (¼ cup)
½ pound ripe tomatoes, seeded and diced (1 cup)
1 garlic clove, minced
2 scallions, minced (¼ cup)
⅓ cup fresh lime juice
½ tablespoon cumin seed, toasted and crushed
1 chipotle chile en adobo, finely chopped
1 small shallot, minced
1 teaspoon raw sugar (optional)
½ teaspoon salt
⅛ teaspoon freshly ground black pepper
⅔ cup canola oil

Combine beans, corn, onion, tomatoes, garlic, and scallions in a large bowl. Whisk together remaining ingredients, adding oil in a thin stream to make an emulsion. Pour the dressing over the vegetables and mix thoroughly. Add salt and pepper to taste. *Yield: 3½ cups.*

Black-Eyed Pea and Corn Salsa

This is a great appetizer salsa served with toast rounds. It's also good with baked ham, especially on New Year's Day! It's substantial enough to serve over greens as a main course. Use fresh black-eyed peas if you can get them. Otherwise, frozen, canned, or dried peas (cooked before you use them, of course) are a good substitute. This salsa keeps well in the refrigerator for up to a week.

1 cup cooked black-eyed peas, drained
1 cup fresh corn kernels, cooked (or frozen
    kernels, thawed)
3 celery stalks, finely diced (½ cup)
1 medium red bell pepper, seeded and finely diced
    (1 cup)
3 scallions, chopped (⅓ cup)
3 tablespoons balsamic vinegar
2 teaspoons honey
1 teaspoon grainy prepared Dijon mustard
½ teaspoon salt
1 pinch freshly ground black pepper
¼ cup canola oil

Combine vegetables in a large bowl and toss well. Whisk remaining ingredients together while adding oil in a thin stream to make an emulsion. Pour the dressing over the vegetables. Chill for 1 hour. Add salt and pepper to taste. *Yield: About 3 cups.*

Herbed Chile Salsa

We love the fresh aroma and the chile sizzle of this fragrant hot salsa. Spread it on steaks as they come off the grill, or use it to decorate a cold poached fish or a roasted duck. It keeps well for several days in the refrigerator.

*2 large poblano chiles, roasted, peeled, seeded,
    and diced (see pages 176–77)*
*1 large pickled jalapeño chile, seeded and
    finely diced*
1 large fresh serrano chile, seeded and minced
½ small red onion, finely chopped (½ cup)
2 garlic cloves, minced
¼ cup fresh cilantro leaves, chopped
¼ cup fresh parsley, chopped
2 tablespoons fresh oregano leaves, minced
2 tablespoons fresh basil leaves, minced
1 tablespoon fresh mint leaves, minced
1 teaspoon white wine vinegar
1 tablespoon fresh lime juice
2 tablespoons olive oil

Combine ingredients thoroughly and chill for an hour. Add salt and pepper to taste. *Yield: About 1 ¼ cups.*

Sesame Cucumber Salsa

This refreshing Asian-style salsa goes beautifully with spicy fish tacos or grilled salmon. We also like it scooped up with crisp, salty tortilla chips. Serve it within a few hours of assembling.

*2 medium cucumbers, peeled, seeded, and
    chopped (2 cups)
1 red bell pepper, seeded, and chopped (1 cup)
¼ small red onion, finely chopped (¼ cup)
¼ cup fresh parsley, minced
¼ cup rice wine vinegar
2 teaspoons raw sugar
¼ teaspoon fresh ginger, minced
1 teaspoon sesame oil
½ cup peanut or canola oil*

Combine cucumbers, pepper, onion, and parsley in a large bowl and chill. In a small bowl, whisk together the vinegar, sugar, ginger, and sesame oil, and then whisk in canola oil in a steady stream to make an emulsion. Pour dressing over vegetables and chill for about an hour. Add salt and pepper to taste. *Yield: About 3 cups.*

Greek Salsa

A refreshing salsa with Mediterranean flair, this one goes beautifully with grilled or roasted lamb. It will keep for a day or two in the refrigerator, but may absorb its liquid. If it becomes dry, sprinkle it with a few drops of vinegar and olive oil just before serving.

> *3 Roma tomatoes, seeded, and diced (1 cup)*
> *½ cup Kalamata olives, rinsed, pitted, and*
> *   quartered (about 20)*
> *¼ pound firm feta cheese, finely diced*
> *½ small red onion, finely chopped (½ cup)*
> *4 garlic cloves, peeled and minced*
> *2 tablespoons fresh parsley, minced*
> *2 tablespoons fresh oregano leaves, minced*
> *2 teaspoons fresh thyme leaves, minced*
> *2 teaspoons fresh lemon juice*
> *2 teaspoons balsamic vinegar*
> *3 tablespoons extra virgin olive oil*

Combine ingredients gently, and then cover and chill for an hour. Add salt and pepper to taste. *Yield: About 2½ cups.*

Anchovy Artichoke Salsa

This very Provençal salsa is simple and delicious scooped up with crisp pita toasts or chips, stuffed into mushroom caps or hollowed cherry tomatoes, or piled next to a cold poached fish for a summer supper. As for the *Olive and Artichoke Salsa* (see page 12), we think fresh artichoke hearts (simple to prepare in advance and keep in the refrigerator for a day or two) are essential—use the canned or frozen substitute at your own risk! This salsa keeps well in the refrigerator for several days.

> *4 large artichokes, trimmed*
> *2 tablespoons fresh lemon juice*
> *1 garlic clove, peeled*
> *¼ cup olive oil*
> *1 teaspoon fresh lemon juice*
> *¼ cup fresh parsley leaves, minced*
> *½ cup extra virgin olive oil*
> *8 to 10 anchovy fillets, chopped*
> *1 garlic clove, crushed and minced*

Drop the trimmed artichokes into a large pot of boiling water. Add lemon juice, garlic, and ¼ cup olive oil to the pot and return to a boil. Lower the flame, partially cover the pot, and cook at a vigorous simmer for about 45 minutes. Drain the artichokes and let them cool. Trim away leaves, remove chokes, and finely dice the hearts. You should have about 1 cup of diced artichoke hearts. Place the artichokes in a small, deep glass bowl. Sprinkle with lemon juice and parsley; toss and set aside.

In a small enameled saucepan, heat the ½ cup olive oil over a low flame to warm but not hot. Add the anchovy fillets to the oil and mash them with the back of a wooden spoon until they are thoroughly mixed into the oil. Stir in the garlic and let the mixture cool to lukewarm. Pour the anchovy oil over the artichokes and toss well. Let stand at least an hour for flavors to meld. Add salt and pepper to taste. Serve at room temperature.
Yield: About 1¼ cups.

Olive and Artichoke Salsa

This substantial salsa is like a bowl of Italian antipasto. And it seems to vanish with lightning speed! We serve it on the side with pasta dishes, grilled fish or chicken, and grilled sandwiches. We've been known to stuff it into mushroom caps or croustades for gala occasions. We think fresh artichoke hearts (simple to prepare in advance and keep in the refrigerator for a day or two) are essential for this salsa—use the canned or frozen substitute at your own risk! It keeps well in the refrigerator for several days.

4 large artichokes, trimmed
2 tablespoons fresh lemon juice
1 garlic clove, peeled
¼ cup olive oil
2 Roma tomatoes, seeded, and diced (⅔ cup)
½ cup brine-cured black olives, rinsed, pitted, and chopped
3 ounces hard Italian salami, finely diced
3 tablespoons Parmesan cheese, grated
2 garlic cloves, crushed and minced
3 tablespoons fresh parsley, chopped
2 tablespoons fresh basil leaves, minced
1 tablespoon capers, drained
½ teaspoon fennel seeds, crushed
2 tablespoons red wine vinegar
1 tablespoon balsamic vinegar
¼ cup virgin olive oil

Drop the trimmed artichokes into a large pot of boiling water. Add lemon juice, garlic, and olive oil to the pot and return to a boil. Lower the flame, partially cover the pot, and cook at a vigorous simmer for about 45 minutes. Drain the artichokes and let them cool. Trim away leaves, remove chokes, and dice the hearts. You should have about 1 cup of diced artichoke hearts.

Mix the artichoke hearts with remaining ingredients and chill for an hour or more to meld flavors. Add salt and pepper to taste. *Yield: About 3 cups.*

Sweet Tomatillo and Chile Salsa

Serve this unusual spicy salsa with grilled or roasted meats, with chicken salad, or with paper-thin slices of jicama or turnip for scooping. It's a zingy garnish for sandwiches, too. It keeps well in the refrigerator for up to a week.

1 pound fresh tomatillos, chopped (2 cups)
2 large green apples, chopped (2 cups)
2 poblano chiles, roasted, peeled, seeded,
*   and chopped (see pages 176–77)*
1 small white onion, chopped (½ cup)
⅓ cup golden raisins
⅓ cup piñon nuts, lightly toasted
⅓ cup raw sugar
⅓ cup strong brewed coffee
1½ tablespoons apple cider vinegar
½ teaspoon fresh lemon zest
½ teaspoon fresh orange zest
⅛ teaspoon grated nutmeg
¼ teaspoon salt

Combine ingredients in a heavy saucepan and bring to a simmer over medium flame. Reduce flame and barely simmer for 15 minutes, stirring frequently. Cool, taste for seasoning, and add salt and pepper if you like. *Yield: About 3 cups.*

Winter Salsa with Chipotle Chile

This winter salsa, similar to a hot vegetable relish, is a nice accompaniment to baked or grilled fish, and we love it scooped up with salty tortilla chips, too. It keeps well in the refrigerator for several days.

4 tablespoons olive oil
1 small yellow onion, chopped (1 cup)
1 yellow bell pepper, chopped (1 cup)
½ cup fresh orange juice
1 teaspoon fresh lime zest
1 tablespoon chipotle en adobo, minced
9 Roma tomatoes, seeded and chopped (3 cups)
1 small red bell pepper, chopped (¾ cup)
1½ tablespoons fresh lime juice
2 tablespoons fresh cilantro leaves, chopped
1 11-ounce can mandarin orange sections, drained

In a large skillet, sauté onion and yellow bell pepper in 2 tablespoons of the olive oil over medium-high flame until vegetables are tender, or about 4 minutes. Stir orange juice, lime zest, and chipotle into onion mixture, turn off the flame, and cool. Add tomatoes and red bell pepper to the cooled onion mixture.

Puree ¼ cup of the cooked vegetables in a food processor while slowly adding the remaining 2 tablespoons of olive oil. Stir the puree back into the vegetables, add lime juice, cilantro, and mandarin orange sections, and mix thoroughly. Add salt and pepper to taste. *Yield: 5 cups.*

Roasted Corn and Red Pepper Salsa

This piquant cooked salsa is reminiscent of the corn relish that appeared on Grandmother's table at holiday time. We've cut the sugar and sparked it with Southwest chile flavor, and we enjoy it all year round. It's good with cold meats and cheeses, and great with barbecue. If you can't get fresh corn for roasting, you can substitute canned or frozen kernels. It keeps well in the refrigerator for a week or more.

> *2 large ears fresh corn, unhusked (or 1½ cups of kernels)*
> *1 large red bell pepper, roasted, peeled, seeded, and*
> *   chopped (see pages 176–77) (1 cup)*
> *2 poblano chiles, roasted, peeled, seeded, and chopped*
> *   (see pages 176–77)*
> *½ small red onion, finely chopped (½ cup)*
> *1 small zucchini, finely chopped (½ cup)*
> *1 large tomato, peeled, seeded, and chopped (1 cup)*
> *½ cup white wine*
> *½ cup white wine vinegar*
> *3 tablespoons raw sugar*
> *½ teaspoon ground cumin*
> *½ teaspoon dried rosemary*
> *½ teaspoon hot red chile powder*
> *1 teaspoon salt*
> *½ cup water chestnuts, peeled and chopped*

Roast the ears of corn in their husks over a charcoal grill or in a hot oven (500 degrees F) for 20 to 30 minutes and allow them to cool. Husk the ears, cut the corn from the cobs, and mix with remaining chopped vegetables.

In a large saucepan, boil the wine, vinegar, sugar, cumin, rosemary, chile powder, and salt for 5 minutes. Stir in the vegetables, lower the flame, and simmer the salsa for 20 minutes. Cool the mixture. Add pepper and more salt to taste. Stir in the water chestnuts and chill. *Yield: About 3½ cups.*

Chipotle Vegetable Salsa

It just wouldn't be a picnic without a big bowl of this zesty salsa and plenty of chips or pita toasts. The heat is Southwest, but the savory is pure South—so serve it with baked ham, pork chops, or anything you put on the barbecue grill. It keeps well in the refrigerator for a week or more.

> *½ pound carrots, finely diced (1 cup)*
> *½ pound zucchini, finely diced (1 cup)*
> *¼ pound green beans, chopped (½ cup)*
> *¼ pound jicama, peeled and finely diced (½ cup)*
> *½ green bell pepper, minced (⅓ cup)*
> *½ small red onion, minced (⅓ cup)*
> *¾ cup tomato juice*
> *2 tablespoons chipotle en adobo, minced*
> *⅓ cup brown sugar*
> *¼ cup apple cider vinegar*
> *1½ tablespoons white wine vinegar*
> *3 tablespoons olive oil*
> *1 tablespoon Worcestershire sauce*
> *1 tablespoon dark brown mustard*
> *½ tablespoon soy sauce*
> *½ teaspoon salt*

Steam the carrots, zucchini, and green beans just until tender-crunchy, and then plunge the vegetables into ice water to stop the cooking. Drain the vegetables and set aside in a large glass bowl with the jicama.

Whisk the remaining ingredients together in a heavy saucepan and bring to a boil over medium flame. Reduce the flame and simmer the sauce for 30 minutes while stirring frequently. Let the sauce cool to just warm, and then pour over the diced vegetables. Cover and chill the salsa for 2 or 3 days before serving. Add pepper and more salt to taste. *Yield: About 3 cups.*

Pineapple Raspberry Salsa

Sweet and savory, cool and hot—this fresh fruit salsa is a hit with chicken, turkey, or baked ham, and as a side dressing for grilled sandwiches. We also like it tucked into half an avocado placed on mixed greens for a special luncheon. It's best served within a few hours of assembling.

1 cup fresh pineapple, finely chopped and well drained
1 cup fresh raspberries, rinsed and dried
¼ small red onion, finely chopped (¼ cup)
¼ cup peeled water chestnuts, chopped
1 fresh jalapeño chile, seeded and minced
½ cup fresh cilantro leaves, finely chopped
¼ cup fresh mint leaves, finely chopped
2 teaspoons raspberry vinegar
2 tablespoons fresh lime juice
⅓ cup canola oil

Combine ingredients in a large bowl. Mix gently and chill about an hour. Add salt and pepper to taste. *Yield: About 2½ cups.*

CRUNCH!

Texture is right up there with aroma, flavor, and color for triggering our responses to food. Especially in cold salsas and slaws, we think a little crunch is guaranteed to enhance the total experience. If your dish looks good and tastes great but needs a little textural character for it to wake up and sing, toss in some crunch, such as diced or slivered raw carrot, celery, radish, cauliflower, broccoli, fennel, bell pepper, water chestnut, jicama, bean sprouts, turnip, apple, nuts, coconut, pickle . . .

Fresh Mango and Red Pepper Salsa

This beautiful fresh fruit salsa couldn't be simpler to make. It goes well with all kinds of seafood and with chicken hot off the grill. It will turn a little soupy if it sits too long, so toss it together just before serving.

2 cups fresh mango, diced
1 cup fresh pineapple, diced and drained
½ cup red bell pepper, finely diced
½ cup Vidalia or sweet onion, finely diced
1 garlic clove, minced
1 fresh serrano chile, seeded and minced
2 tablespoons fresh mint leaves, minced

Combine ingredients and chill for an hour. Add salt and pepper to taste. *Yield: About 3½ cups.*

Sweet Cherry Salsa

We freshen the flavor of dark sweet cherries with lime zest and steep them in aromatic cilantro to produce this elegant salsa for dressing up pork or fowl. If you're able to get fresh cherries, so much the better. The salsa will keep chilled for up to a week—but only if you don't tell anyone where you've hidden it!

1 16-ounce package frozen bing cherries
3 teaspoons fresh lime juice
¼ teaspoon fresh lime zest
2 tablespoons scallion, finely chopped
1½ teaspoons fresh jalapeño chile, seeded and minced
2 tablespoons fresh cilantro leaves, finely chopped
⅓ cup honey

Defrost and drain the cherries, and pit them if necessary. Mix the drained cherries with lime juice and zest, and then stir in the remaining ingredients. Chill the salsa for 24 hours, stirring occasionally. Add salt and pepper to taste. *Yield: About 2 cups.*

Fiery Tropical Salsa

This sparkling fresh salsa is marvelous with grilled or poached fish or cold sliced chicken or turkey, and can be varied to suit the season or your mood. The combination of fresh blueberries, kiwifruit, and mangoes is spectacular. Assemble and chill for only an hour or two before serving.

>*2½ cups fresh berries or diced tropical fruits, or a mix*
>*¼ cup yellow bell pepper, diced*
>*¼ cup red bell pepper, diced*
>*¼ cup water chestnuts, diced*
>*1 bunch small scallions, diced*
>*1 tablespoon fresh cilantro leaves, minced (or more, if you love it)*
>*2 fresh jalapeño chiles, seeded and minced*
>*¼ cup raw sugar*
>*2 tablespoons shredded coconut meat, unsweetened*
>*2 tablespoons white wine vinegar*

Gently mix the ingredients together in a glass bowl and toss lightly, being careful not to bruise the fruit. Chill an hour or two to meld flavors. *Yield: About 3 cups.*

Peach Berry Salsa

What could be simpler or more refreshing on a summer evening? We love this fresh fruit salsa with baked ham, fried chicken, or grilled fish. Serve it within a few hours of assembling.

2 large firm peaches
2 tablespoons fresh lemon juice
½ cup small, fresh strawberries, washed, hulled,
*   and quartered*
½ cup small, fresh blueberries, washed and dried
¼ small red onion, finely chopped (¼ cup)
1 fresh serrano chile, seeded and minced
2 tablespoons almonds, skinned, toasted, and chopped
2 tablespoons fresh parsley, minced
2 teaspoons fresh ginger, minced
½ teaspoon curry powder
1 tablespoon raspberry vinegar
⅓ cup canola oil

Peel the peaches and finely dice them, and then toss with lemon juice and set aside. Combine remaining ingredients gently, stir in the peaches, and chill for an hour. Add salt and pepper to taste.
Yield: About 2½ cups.

Watermelon Mint Salsa

This salsa will refresh the most wilted guests on a summer evening. We serve it with salty tortilla chips, or packed into hollowed cucumber cups for snazzy occasions, or as a side dressing for whatever is coming off the grill. Put it together just before serving—it will turn into watermelon soup if you let it sit too long. (Hmm, watermelon soup! Doesn't sound like a bad idea…)

> 1½ cups firm watermelon, seeded and finely diced
> ½ cup kiwifruit, peeled and finely diced
> ¼ small red onion, finely chopped (¼ cup)
> 1 fresh serrano chile, seeded and minced
> ½ cup fresh mint leaves, minced
> 3 teaspoons white wine vinegar
> 2 teaspoons fresh lime juice
> ¼ cup canola oil

Put diced watermelon in a large colander and let drain at least 30 minutes. Roll up in a clean dish towel and chill. Meanwhile, combine remaining ingredients, mix thoroughly, and chill for about an hour. Just before serving, stir watermelon into the salsa and mix gently. Add salt and pepper to taste. *Yield: About 2 cups.*

Grapefruit and Avocado Salsa

This popular combination of rich avocado and tangy grapefruit is a natural for summer at the shore. It's delightful with any broiled fish or other seafood. We also love it scooped up on salty tortilla chips or pita toast, rolled into crisp leaves of butter lettuce, or piled on cold poached sea bass. It should be served immediately after preparation.

> *2 large red-fleshed grapefruits*
> *1 firm (but ripe!) Haas avocado*
> *3 radishes, scrubbed and finely chopped*
> *1 fresh serrano chile, seeded and minced*
> *1 tablespoon fresh parsley, chopped*
> *1 tablespoon fresh cilantro, chopped*
> *1 teaspoon fresh lime juice*
> *1 teaspoon red wine vinegar*
> *½ teaspoon ground cumin*
> *1 tablespoon avocado or canola oil*

Peel the grapefruit with a sharp knife, cutting away all the pith and membrane. Carefully section the fruit, and then chop gently into small pieces. Set the grapefruit pieces aside in a bowl with their juices. Peel and seed the avocado. Cut the flesh into small dice and gently stir into the grapefruit pieces. Combine radishes with remaining ingredients, cover, and chill. Just before serving, drain the grapefruit and avocado thoroughly, and then toss gently with the dressed radishes. Add salt and pepper to taste. *Yield: About 2 cups.*

Apple and Blue Cheese Salsa

We love this rich salsa with beef—hot or cold. We also serve it
rolled up in leaves of butter lettuce; stuffed into roasted
jalapeños, which we then batter and fry; or mounded on spicy
pita crisps. Fresh apples wimp out pretty quickly, so the salsa is
best served the day you make it.

> *1 large green apple, chopped (1 cup)*
> *1 large red apple, chopped (1 cup)*
> *2 teaspoons fresh lemon juice*
> *¼ small red onion, finely chopped (¼ cup)*
> *⅓ cup Hot Chile Walnuts (see page 181)*
> *½ cup blue cheese, crumbled*
> *2 tablespoons white wine vinegar*
> *¼ teaspoon red chile powder*
> *¼ teaspoon salt*
> *2 tablespoons fresh parsley, minced*
> *2 tablespoons walnut oil*
> *2 tablespoons canola oil*

Toss the apples with the lemon juice as you chop to prevent
darkening. Combine apple, onion, walnuts, and blue cheese in a
large bowl. Whisk remaining ingredients together, adding oils in a
steady stream to make an emulsion. Pour dressing over the salsa,
mix gently, and chill for an hour. Add salt and pepper to taste.
Yield: About 3 cups.

Pear and Fennel Salsa

This salsa, a delicate one spiced with aromatic ginger and fennel, is exceptionally good with cold roasted chicken or turkey. We also roll it in leaves of butter lettuce as an appetizer, and serve it with rich biscotti and cheese after dinner. The salsa should be served within two or three hours of assembling.

> 1 large Bartlett pear, cored and diced (about 1½ cups)
> 2 teaspoons fresh lemon juice
> ¼ cup fennel bulb, finely diced
> ¼ cup celery (inner stalks), finely diced
> ¼ cup Ginger Soy Walnuts, chopped (see page 183)
> 1 tablespoon fresh parsley, minced
> ½ tablespoon fresh ginger, minced
> ½ teaspoon fennel seeds, crushed
> 2 teaspoons white wine vinegar
> 1 tablespoon walnut oil
> 2 tablespoons peanut or canola oil

Toss the diced pear with the lemon juice and set aside. Combine remaining ingredients thoroughly, stir in the diced pear, and chill for about an hour. Add salt and pepper to taste. *Yield: About 2 cups.*

Spiked Cranberry Apple Salsa

This zesty accompaniment for pork or chicken is also delicious with sliced cold meats and cheeses, or with salty chips for scooping. It's simple to chop together in a food processor—just be careful not to reduce it to mush! It keeps well in the refrigerator for up to a week.

1 poblano chile, roasted, peeled, seeded, and chopped
    (see pages 176–77)
1 cup raw cranberries, chopped
1 medium green apple, chopped (1 cup)
½ medium orange, chopped (½ cup)
⅓ cup Hot Chile Pecans, roughly chopped (see page 181)
⅓ cup raw sugar
¼ teaspoon ground cloves
⅛ teaspoon ground cumin
2 tablespoons dark tequila

Combine ingredients thoroughly and chill for an hour. Add salt and pepper to taste. Refrigerate for a day or two before serving to develop flavors. *Yield: About 3 cups.*

Spiced Melon Salsa

Fresh cilantro lends the authentic flavor of Mexico and the Southwest to this cool, spicy fruit salsa. It's a delight with salty tortilla chips, and is also a refreshing complement to grilled chicken or seafood. It keeps well for several days in the refrigerator.

¾ cup water
½ cup white wine
⅓ cup white wine vinegar
1 whole pickled jalapeño chile
12 whole cloves
⅓ cup raw sugar
½ cantaloupe, cut in spears 1 inch wide
⅓ honeydew melon, cut in spears 1 inch wide
½ small red onion, finely chopped (½ cup)
1 small jicama, peeled and finely diced (1 cup)
1 fresh serrano chile, seeded and minced
3 tablespoons fresh cilantro leaves, minced
⅛ teaspoon salt

Combine water, wine, vinegar, jalapeño, cloves, and sugar in a medium saucepan. Bring mixture to a boil, and then lower the flame and simmer about 5 minutes. Add the melon spears and bring the mixture back to a boil, and then remove from the flame, and cool. Chill the melon overnight in the spiced liquid.

To assemble the salsa, remove the melon spears from the liquid, discard the pulpy inner layer of the honeydew spears, and finely dice the melon. You should have about 2½ cups of diced melon. Combine melon with remaining ingredients and drizzle with enough spiced liquid to moisten. Chill the salsa for an hour. Add salt and pepper to taste. *Yield: About 4 cups.*

Dried Cranberry Salsa

This sweet but tangy-hot salsa is nice to have on hand to dress up sandwiches or grilled fish or poultry, or to enjoy with salty tortilla chips or pita crisps. We've been known to mix it with fresh apples to fill a holiday pie! Chilled, it keeps well for up to two weeks.

1 teaspoon olive oil
½ medium red bell pepper, finely diced (½ cup)
1 fresh jalapeño chile, seeded and minced
½ large red onion, finely diced (1 cup)
¼ cup brown sugar, packed
1 tablespoon fresh ginger, grated
1 large garlic clove, minced
½ cup currants
1 cup dried cranberries
zest and juice of 1 orange
¼ teaspoon Coleman's dry mustard
½ teaspoon red chile powder
¼ cup red wine vinegar
½ cup green apple, finely diced

In a large stainless steel or enamel saucepan, heat the oil and sauté the red pepper, jalapeño, and onion, with the ginger, garlic, and 2 teaspoons of the brown sugar. Simmer the mixture over a medium flame while stirring until the vegetables are wilted, or about 6 minutes. Stir in all remaining ingredients except the diced apple and cook 10 minutes. Add the apple and cook about 5 minutes. Cool the salsa, taste for seasoning and add salt and pepper if you like. *Yield: About 4 cups.*

Winter Fruit Salsa

Rich and pungent, this combination of nuts and dried fruit with fresh apple and crunchy fennel is a marvelous dressing for roasted meats, stuffing for holiday chiles rellenos, or filling for festive tarts or turnovers. It turns your bag-lunch smoked turkey sandwich into manna from heaven. Use a combination of dried pears, apricots, figs, cherries, cranberries, raisins, or whatever you like best. It keeps well in the refrigerator for a week or more.

½ cup white wine vinegar
½ cup raw sugar
1 cup mixed dried fruits, chopped
¼ small red onion, finely chopped (¼ cup)
½ lemon, finely chopped
½ orange, finely chopped
1 tablespoon fresh ginger, minced
¼ teaspoon ground cinnamon
¼ teaspoon ground cloves
¼ teaspoon red chile powder
¼ teaspoon salt
1 tablespoon brandy
1 large green apple, finely chopped (1 cup)
⅓ cup fennel bulb, finely chopped
⅓ cup Winter Spiced Walnuts, roughly chopped
    (see page 182)

Combine all ingredients except apple, fennel and walnuts in a large heavy saucepan. Bring to a boil over medium flame. Reduce the flame and simmer the mixture gently 30 to 40 minutes, while adding a little more water or wine when and if the mixture becomes too dry. Cool to room temperature and then chill. Before serving, stir in apple, fennel, and walnuts. Add pepper and more salt if you like. *Yield: About 2½ cups.*

 Sauces

Cilantro Lime Pesto

This delicious concoction has a cool and fresh taste and is a nice change from traditional basil pestos. Serve it over fresh steamed clams or mussels, add it to bouillabaisse, or mix with your favorite pasta. Covered with a coating of olive oil, it keeps well in the refrigerator for several days.

> 1 bunch fresh cilantro, washed, dried, and stemmed
>   (1 cup packed)
> 1 cup fresh parsley, chopped
> ½ cup Romano cheese, grated
> ¼ cup shelled pistachio nuts, toasted
> 1 tablespoon fresh ginger, chopped
> 1 fresh jalapeño chile, seeded and chopped
> zest of 1 lime
> 4 garlic cloves, crushed
> ¼ cup olive oil

Combine all ingredients except oil in a food processor and pulse to blend. With processor going, add the oil in a stream until pesto is just pureed. Do not overprocess; the pesto should retain some character. Add salt and pepper if you wish. *Yield: 3½ cups.*

Spicy Spinach Pesto

A little lingering heat makes this pesto a winner on pasta, in an omelet, on a grilled sandwich, or just for dipping. If you want more fire, toss in another serrano chile. Covered with a coating of olive oil, the pesto keeps well in the refrigerator for up to a week.

½ cup fresh spinach leaves, washed, trimmed, and
  tightly packed
½ cup fresh basil leaves, washed and tightly packed
¼ cup walnuts, lightly toasted
2 garlic cloves, peeled and chopped
1 fresh serrano chile, seeded and chopped
½ cup Parmesan cheese, grated
¼ teaspoon salt
½ teaspoon fresh lemon juice
1 pinch grated nutmeg
½ cup extra virgin olive oil

Combine ingredients in food processor and pulse to a thick, rough puree. Add more olive oil if sauce is too thick. Do not overprocess; the pesto should retain some character. Add salt and pepper if you wish. *Yield: About 1¼ cups.*

Arugula and Asiago Pesto

This robust and peppery pesto is wonderful with pasta, and we love it spread on crusty bread or as a dip for pita toast. Be sure to use tender baby arugula or the pesto will turn bitter. Covered with a coating of olive oil, it will keep refrigerated for up to a week.

*½ cup baby arugula, washed, trimmed,
   and tightly packed*
*¼ cup fresh parsley, washed, stemmed,
   and tightly packed*
¼ cup fresh basil leaves, tightly packed
2 garlic cloves, chopped
¼ cup piñon nuts, lightly toasted
¼ cup Asiago cheese, shredded
½ cup olive oil

Combine ingredients in food processor and pulse to a coarse puree. Add more olive oil if sauce is too thick. Do not overprocess; the pesto should retain some rough texture. Add salt and pepper if you wish. *Yield: 1¼ cups.*

Gazpacho Sauce

Use the freshest ingredients for this chunky, refreshing sauce that smells and tastes like it just came out of the summer garden. We serve it with shrimp or fish right off the grill, or as a dressing for cold poached seafood or composed vegetable salads. It keeps well in the refrigerator for several days.

> *3 ½ tablespoons virgin olive oil*
> *1 fresh garlic clove, minced*
> *¼ small yellow onion, diced (¼ cup)*
> *½ medium red bell pepper, seeded and chopped (½ cup)*
> *½ medium cucumber, peeled, seeded, and*
>   *chopped (½ cup)*
> *1 fresh jalapeño chile, seeded and minced*
> *¼ teaspoon salt*
> *½ pound ripe tomatoes, seeded and chopped (1 cup)*
> *2 tablespoons fresh parsley, chopped*
> *½ cup fresh cilantro leaves, chopped*

In a medium saucepan, heat ½ tablespoon of the olive oil over a medium flame. Add garlic, onion, red pepper, cucumber, jalapeño, and salt to the pan and cook 3 to 4 minutes. Add tomatoes, parsley, and cilantro to the sauce, bring to a simmer, and cook for 10 minutes. Add remaining oil to the sauce and cool. Add salt and pepper if you wish. *Yield: About 2 cups.*

Anchovy Olive Sauce

A tapenade made with anchovies, this thick sauce is rich, salty, and powerful. We love it spread on crusty bread, and as a side dressing for cheese soufflé, scrambled eggs, pasta, or grilled vegetables. It keeps well in the refrigerator for up to a week (if it's well hidden!).

> 1 2-ounce can flat anchovy fillets, drained
> ½ cup brine-cured black olives, rinsed,
>   pitted, and chopped
> 2 garlic cloves, peeled and chopped
> 4 tablespoons fresh parsley, chopped
> ⅛ teaspoon red chile powder
> 2 teaspoons fresh lemon juice
> 1 tablespoon white wine
> ¼ cup extra virgin olive oil

Combine ingredients in food processor and pulse to a coarse puree, adding more olive oil by the spoonful until sauce is desired consistency. Do not overprocess; sauce should retain some rough texture. Add salt and pepper if you wish. *Yield: About ¾ cup.*

Red Horseradish Sauce

Horseradish is great with beef, of course, whether hot or cold. We also love this fresh, zingy tomato sauce as a hot or cold dressing for cheese soufflé, omelets, spinach quiche, grilled sandwiches, or broiled fish. When chilled, it keeps well for several days.

> *6 Roma tomatoes, peeled, seeded, and pureed*
>   *(about 1 cup)*
> *¼ small red onion, grated (3 or 4 tablespoons)*
> *2 teaspoons fresh horseradish, grated*
> *2 tablespoons fresh parsley, minced*
> *1 garlic clove, minced*
> *1 teaspoon white wine vinegar*
> *1 tablespoon olive oil*

Pour the pureed tomato into a sieve lined with two layers of damp cheesecloth and set aside to drain for 30 minutes. Whisk remaining ingredients into the drained puree and chill for an hour. Add salt and pepper if you wish. *Yield: About 1¼ cups.*

Red Chile Sauce

This is an earthy, typically northern New Mexican red chile sauce, an everyday staple throughout the Southwest. It's an authentic, robust sauce for enchiladas, huevos rancheros, or grilled steaks. It keeps well in the refrigerator for a week or more, and freezes beautifully.

½ cup pure red chile powder
2½ cups vegetable or chicken stock (or water)
2 or 3 tablespoons canola oil
1 small white onion, finely chopped (1 cup)
2 garlic cloves, finely chopped
1 teaspoon cumin seed, toasted and ground
1 teaspoon dried oregano
⅛ teaspoon ground cinnamon
1 teaspoon salt

Put the chile powder in a medium bowl and whisk 1 cup of the broth or water into the powder to make a smooth mixture with no lumps, and then set aside.

Heat the oil in a large heavy saucepan and sauté the onion in it for 5 minutes over a medium flame. Toss in the garlic and sauté another 2 minutes. Stir in the cumin, oregano and cinnamon and cook, stirring constantly, for 2 minutes. Scrape the chile mixture into the pan and stir, and then add the remaining broth or water and cook, stirring, until the sauce reaches the simmering point. Do not let the chile scorch. Reduce the flame to low and simmer the sauce gently, still stirring frequently, for 20 to 30 minutes or until it is the consistency you like. Set aside to cool. *Yield: About 2 cups.*

San Miguel Red Sauce

This is a typical sauce of central Mexico, made with whole dried ancho, pasilla, and mulato chiles (see page 178). It is a very dark, rich sauce with earthy flavor, medium heat, and the slightest touch of aromatic spice. We love it with pork or bean stews, with roasted or grilled meats, or as a sauce for enchiladas or huevos rancheros. It keeps in the refrigerator for a week or more, and freezes beautifully.

2 ½ cups chicken or beef stock
5 pasilla chiles
3 ancho chiles
3 mulato chiles
4 tablespoons lard (or oil)
1 medium white onion, chopped (1 cup)
3 garlic cloves, peeled and chopped
2 tablespoons blanched almonds, toasted and ground
½ teaspoon cumin seeds, toasted and ground
⅛ teaspoon ground cinnamon
⅛ teaspoon ground cloves
½ teaspoon salt

Bring the stock to a simmer over a medium flame, then reduce the heat and keep the stock hot.

Wipe the chiles with a damp cloth and remove the stems and seeds. In a large, heavy skillet, heat the lard to hot, but not smoking, and fry the chiles, turning frequently to prevent scorching, until they are soft and very dark. Remove the chiles with a slotted spoon to the bowl of a food processor. Add the chopped onion and garlic to the skillet and sauté while stirring for 2 minutes. Add the onion and garlic to the chiles.

Add ¼ cup of the hot beef stock to the chiles and process to a puree, adding more stock as necessary to achieve a thick but fairly smooth mixture. Return the skillet to the range over medium flame, and when the remaining lard is hot, but not smoking, scrape the puree into the skillet.

Fry the puree for 2 or 3 minutes, stirring constantly to keep the chiles from scorching. (They will spatter a lot, so be careful.)

Whisk the remaining hot stock into the chile mixture, then toss in the ground almonds, cumin, cinnamon, cloves, and salt. Simmer the sauce, stirring occasionally, for 20 to 30 minutes. If the sauce is too thick, add stock. Add salt and pepper if you wish. *Yield: About 3 cups.*

Green Chile Tomatillo Sauce

This fresh, piquant green sauce is ideal for chicken enchiladas. We also use it as a side dressing for tacos, quesadillas, omelets, and grilled fish or chicken. It keeps well in the refrigerator for a week or more, and freezes beautifully.

> *½ medium white onion, finely chopped (½ cup)*
> *4 garlic cloves, minced*
> *3 tablespoons lard or oil*
> *1 pound fresh tomatillos, chopped (2 cups)*
> *1 pound New Mexico or Anaheim green chiles,*
> *   roasted, peeled, seeded, and chopped (see pages*
> *   176–77)*
> *½ cup water*
> *2 tablespoons raw sugar*
> *2 tablespoons apple cider vinegar*
> *¼ teaspoon salt*

In a heavy saucepan sauté onion and garlic in lard until soft, or about 7 minutes. Stir in remaining ingredients and simmer for 30 minutes. Allow to cool and pass through a ricer or coarse sieve. Add salt and pepper if you wish. *Yield: About 2½ cups.*

Texas Barbecue Sauce

This is a great standard for down-home beef, pork, or chicken barbecue—Texas style. We also keep some handy for jazzing up hamburgers or grilled sandwiches. It keeps in the refrigerator for up to a week and freezes well.

> *4 tablespoons bacon drippings or oil*
> *1 medium yellow onion, finely chopped (1 cup)*
> *4 large garlic cloves, minced*
> *1 red bell pepper, seeded and finely chopped (1 cup)*
> *2 pickled jalapeño chiles, seeded and minced*
> *¾ cup ketchup*
> *¼ cup prepared mustard*
> *1 cup water*
> *½ cup strong brewed coffee*
> *¼ cup apple cider vinegar*
> *2 tablespoons Worcestershire sauce*
> *⅓ cup dark brown sugar, packed*
> *1 teaspoon ground cumin*
> *1 teaspoon red chile powder (or to taste)*
> *½ teaspoon salt*
> *¼ teaspoon freshly ground black pepper*

In a saucepan, sauté onion, garlic, bell pepper, and jalapeño chiles in drippings until wilted, or about 10 minutes. Whisk in remaining ingredients and simmer about an hour. Cool to room temperature and then taste for seasoning. Add more salt and pepper if you wish. *Yield: About 2½ cups.*

Red Bourbon Sauce

This easy no-cook bourbon sauce, hot with mustard and chiles, has a sensational fragrance and takes to all kinds of meats for grilling. We also like it with pan-seared steaks, lamb chops and pork chops. It keeps well in the refrigerator for several days.

¾ cup prepared Dijon-style prepared mustard
¾ cup ketchup
1 or 2 tablespoons ancho or pasilla chile puree
    (see pages 178–79)
½ to ¾ cup raw sugar
½ to ¾ cup bourbon
½ cup soy sauce
1 bunch scallions, finely chopped
3 tablespoons fresh rosemary leaves, finely minced

Beat the mustard, ketchup and chile puree together in a medium bowl. In another bowl, stir the sugar into the bourbon and soy sauce until it is dissolved, and then whisk it into the mustard mixture until well combined. Stir in the scallions and rosemary, and taste for seasoning. Add salt and pepper if you wish, and a dash of red hot pepper sauce if it isn't hot enough for you. Chill the sauce, covered, for an hour or two before using. *Yield: About 2½ cups of sauce.*

Carolina Barbecue Sauce

This traditional vinegar barbecue sauce from the deep South turns slow-cooked pork or beef into manna from heaven! Cook a brisket or pork loin or shoulder for 8 to 10 hours until tender, shred the meat with forks, and steep it in vinegar sauce. The sauce will keep in the refrigerator for several weeks.

1 cup vinegar
¼ cup honey
½ teaspoon freshly ground black pepper
¼ teaspoon salt
¼ teaspoon Your Hot Pepper Sauce (see page 42)

Combine ingredients in a saucepan and simmer about 15 minutes over a medium flame. Taste for seasoning and add more salt and pepper if you wish. *Yield: About 1 cup.*

Oriental Barbecue Sauce

The tangy flavors of soy sauce and fresh ginger make this a great dressing for pork ribs. It's also wonderful as a sandwich spread, or as a dipping sauce for many grilled or deep-fried appetizers from chicken satay to fried wontons. It keeps well for a week or more in the refrigerator.

2 shallots, minced
4 garlic cloves, minced
2 tablespoons peanut oil
1 cup Chile Plum Sauce (see page 44), or bottled
    hoisin sauce
¼ cup soy sauce
½ cup dry sherry
½ cup fresh orange juice
4 tablespoons rice vinegar
2 tablespoons honey
3 tablespoons fresh ginger, minced

In a medium saucepan, sauté shallots and garlic in oil until tender, about 5 minutes. Add remaining ingredients and mix well. Bring to a boil over medium flame, and then lower the flame and simmer the sauce for 20 minutes, stirring occasionally. Let stand to cool to room temperature. Add salt and pepper if you wish. *Yield: About 2 cups.*

Your Hot Pepper Sauce

Once there was Tabasco sauce. Today, there are literally dozens of hot pepper sauces on grocery shelves, and dozens more in specialty shops. You can experiment with making your own—for mere pennies, compared to the cost of the bottled stuff. But remember that hot chile peppers are downright dangerous if not handled with care: wear gloves, protect your eyes from splashes and fumes, and taste cautiously.

Use this basic recipe to make hot sauce from any combination of your favorite chile peppers—habanero, jalapeño, serrano, chipotle, and so on. Flavor and heat will vary by the type of chile peppers you use, whether they are fresh or dried, and whether you include herbs or other flavoring agents. You can vary the amounts of garlic, sugar, and salt to suit your taste; you can try different vinegars; and you can add spices such as cumin or clove. Your sauce should keep for several months in the refrigerator.

> *1 cup hot peppers, fresh or dried, stemmed and seeded*
> *1 or 2 garlic cloves, chopped*
> *2 cups water, or more*
> *½ tablespoon raw sugar*
> *¼ teaspoon salt*
> *½ cup vinegar*

Put the peppers in a heavy, deep saucepan with the garlic and cover with cold water. Bring to a simmer and cook until the peppers are completely soft. Cool the mixture, drain off the water, and force the peppers through a fine sieve. Add remaining ingredients to the pureed peppers. Return mixture to the pot and simmer while stirring for about 10 minutes. Cool, and then pour into a clean glass bottle or jar and refrigerate. *Yield: About ¾ cup.*

Roasted Red Pepper and Tomato Sauce

This chunky, rich tomato sauce is great with pasta, and also shines as a side dressing for grilled fish or sausages, polenta, grilled Jarlsburg cheese sandwiches, stir-fried green beans, and lots of other things. It's best made a day ahead of serving. Use it within a few days, or freeze it.

3 tablespoons olive oil
½ small red onion, finely chopped (½ cup)
8 Roma tomatoes (about 1¼ pounds)
2 garlic cloves, minced
2 red bell peppers, roasted, peeled, seeded, and finely chopped (1 cup) (see pages 176–77)
2 tablespoons fresh parsley, minced
3 teaspoons dried basil
½ teaspoon salt
½ cup vegetable or chicken stock
¼ cup brine-cured black olives, rinsed, pitted, and chopped
⅛ teaspoon crushed red chile flakes

In a large, heavy saucepan, sauté the onion in olive oil until wilted, about 5 minutes. Peel, seed, and puree 5 of the tomatoes; seed and finely dice remaining 3 tomatoes. Add minced garlic to the onions and sauté 1 minute. Add tomato puree, diced tomatoes, and all remaining ingredients to the onions and stir. Bring the sauce to a boil over medium flame; lower the flame and simmer the sauce 20 to 30 minutes. Let stand at room temperature to cool. Add salt and pepper if you wish. *Yield: About 3 cups.*

Chile Plum Sauce

We like the sweet-hot savor of this thick sauce with almost everything! It's a perfect complement to pork, lamb, or turkey (whether served hot or cold); a wonderful sandwich spread; an unusual dressing for poached fruit; and turns Chinese take-out into a feast! It keeps well in the refrigerator for a week or more.

1 pound red plums, pitted (about 2 cups)
1 green apple, roughly chopped (1 cup)
1 pickled jalapeño chile, seeded
1 1-inch piece fresh ginger, peeled and minced
½ cup white wine vinegar
1 tablespoon raw sugar
1 teaspoon ground cinnamon
⅛ teaspoon ground cloves
⅛ teaspoon salt

Combine ingredients in a large enameled saucepan and simmer over medium flame until fruit is very soft, or about 15 minutes. Let the mixture cool, and then put mixture through a ricer or coarse sieve to remove skins. Cover and chill for 2 days for flavors to develop. Add salt and pepper if you wish. *Yield: About 1½ cups.*

Thai Orange Curry Sauce

This is a rich and pungent sauce especially good for dressing pork or chicken. If you cannot locate Thai red curry paste, substitute a teaspoon of your favorite curry powder mixed into a tablespoon of ancho or pasilla chile puree (see pages 178–79). This sauce keeps for several days in the refrigerator, and freezes beautifully.

3 cups fresh orange juice
1 carrot, finely chopped
2 tablespoons fresh cilantro leaves, chopped
2 tablespoons fresh ginger, minced
2 garlic cloves, minced
1 jalapeño chile, seeded and minced
1 tablespoon cumin seeds, toasted and ground
1 tablespoon Thai red curry paste (available in
    Asian markets)
3 to 4 tablespoons unsalted butter

Combine all ingredients except butter in a heavy saucepan over medium flame. Boil the mixture until the carrots are very tender and the liquid is reduced by half, or about 12 minutes. Puree the sauce in a food processor until it is smooth. Strain the sauce through a sieve and return it to the saucepan. Bring the sauce near the simmer over a low flame (don't let it boil), and stir in butter in small pieces, incorporating each piece completely before adding the next. *Yield: About 1½ cups.*

Ginger Garlic Sauce

This pungent sauce is great with baked or broiled chicken. We also use it to marinate shrimp or pork for grilling over hot coals, and as a dipping sauce for baked wontons or deep-fried appetizers. It keeps well in the refrigerator for a week or more.

4 tablespoons fresh ginger, chopped
4 garlic cloves, chopped
½ cup raw sugar
⅓ cup soy sauce
¼ cup rice vinegar
¼ cup ketchup
¼ cup water
3 tablespoons Coleman's dry mustard
1½ teaspoons sesame oil

Combine ingredients in a food processor and blend thoroughly. Add salt and pepper if you wish. *Yield: 2 cups.*

Balsamic Butter Sauce

This easy butter sauce is rich and slightly sweet, a good complement for beef steak, venison, or freshly grilled tuna. We also drizzle it over polenta. It keeps well in the refrigerator for a week or more.

1 cup balsamic vinegar
1 large shallot, minced
4 cups fresh chicken or vegetable stock
1 bay leaf
3 peppercorns
4 tablespoons unsalted butter

In a large, non-reactive saucepan, boil the vinegar and shallot over high flame until reduced to a syrup, or about 10 minutes. Add the stock, bay leaf, and peppercorns. Boil until reduced to 1 cup of thick sauce, or about 15 minutes. Press the hot sauce through a fine sieve, beat in the butter in small pieces until all the butter is incorporated. Cool. Add salt and pepper if you wish. *Yield: 1 cup.*

Balsamic Anchovy Sauce

This potent sauce is a magnificent dressing for cold poached fish, and a marvelous dip for battered and deep-fried fish, chicken pieces, or vegetables. We also love it drizzled over crispy baked polenta. It's easy to make and keeps well in the refrigerator for several days.

5 garlic cloves, crushed and minced
1½ cups fresh parsley leaves, minced
1 cup extra virgin olive oil
8 to 10 anchovy fillets, chopped
¼ cup balsamic vinegar

In a small enameled saucepan, sauté the garlic and parsley over a medium flame in 2 tablespoons of the olive oil until wilted. Pour in remaining olive oil and heat to near simmer. Add the anchovy fillets, mashing them into the oil with the back of a wooden spoon, and cook about 2 minutes. Pour in the vinegar and cook while stirring another 2 or 3 minutes. Cool to warm room temperature before serving. *Yield: 1½ cups.*

Canton Dipping Sauce

We love this as a dipping sauce for dim sum dumplings, fried
wontons, or crispy fried chicken or shrimp. And it makes a great
dressing over fresh mixed greens with some crunch tossed in
(like slivered water chestnuts and almonds). It will keep
refrigerated for up to a month.

⅓ cup water
½ cup soy sauce
¼ cup dry sherry
1 tablespoon raw sugar
1 teaspoon rice vinegar
1 tablespoon green onion, chopped
½ teaspoon garlic, minced

In a small bowl mix all ingredients. Taste for seasoning and add
Your Hot Pepper Sauce (see page 42) if you wish. *Yield: 1½ cups.*

Chile Apple Cider Cream Sauce

Creamy sweet heat is the hallmark of this delicious sauce inspired by a chile relleno dish that originated at Janos Wilder's restaurant in Tucson, Arizona. It's wonderful with pork chops or doves braised with apples. It keeps well in the refrigerator for several days.

> *½ small red onion, finely chopped (½ cup)*
> *1½ cups apple cider*
> *1½ cups white wine*
> *1½ cups heavy cream*
> *1 tablespoon pasilla chile puree (see pages 178–79)*
> *1 tablespoon piñon nuts, lightly toasted*

Bring the onion, cider, and wine to a boil in a large enamel saucepan, and cook until reduced by half (to 1½ cups), or about 10 to 15 minutes. Add the cream, bring to a boil and reduce by half (to 1½ cups), or about 10 to 15 minutes. Pour the sauce through a fine sieve, and then whisk in the chile puree and stir in the nuts. Taste for seasoning and add salt and white pepper if you wish. *Yield: About 1½ cups.*

Ginger Fennel Cream Sauce

A delicate, aromatic sauce, fennel cream is a delicious partner for salmon or for any fine-fleshed white fish. It keeps well in the refrigerator for several days. Rewarm gently over very low flame.

2½ tablespoons shallots, minced
½ tablespoon fresh ginger, minced
1 cup white wine
1 cup heavy cream
1 tablespoon butter
1 medium fennel bulb, trimmed and finely diced (1 cup)
⅛ teaspoon salt

In a small enameled saucepan, vigorously simmer 2 tablespoons of the shallots and ginger in wine over medium flame until reduced to ½ cup, or about 10 minutes. Add the cream and simmer until reduced to 1 cup, or about 10 minutes.

Meanwhile, melt butter in a small skillet over low flame and sauté remaining ½ tablespoon shallots until wilted, or about 3 minutes. Add the diced fennel and sauté until soft, or about 10 minutes. Stir fennel into reduced cream and simmer about 10 minutes. Add salt and pepper if you wish. *Yield: About 1½ cups.*

Sorrel Cream Sauce

This dreamy sauce is easy to make and is wonderful with poached or baked fish or sautéed chicken breasts. It's also a great dressing for pasta primavera with fresh spring vegetables. The sauce can be made up to 24 hours in advance of serving, and rewarmed gently over a low flame.

2½ tablespoons shallots, minced
1 cup white wine
1 cup heavy cream
1 tablespoon butter
½ teaspoon fresh lemon juice
1 cup sorrel leaves, washed, dried, and tightly packed
⅛ teaspoon salt

In a small enamel saucepan, boil 2 tablespoons of the shallots in the wine over medium flame until reduced to ½ cup, or about 10 minutes. Add the cream and continue cooking until reduced to 1 cup, for about 10 to 15 minutes.

Meanwhile, melt butter in a small skillet over low flame and sauté the remaining ½ tablespoon shallots until wilted, or about 3 minutes. Stack sorrel leaves and, with a sharp knife, slice leaves lengthwise into very fine chiffonade. Add sorrel to skillet, sprinkle with lemon juice and salt, and sauté while stirring, about 5 minutes. Stir sorrel into reduced cream and simmer 10 minutes on low flame. Taste for seasoning and add salt and white pepper if you wish. *Yield: About 1½ cups.*

Gorgonzola Cream Sauce

This velvety sauce is richly flavored with blue cheese and walnuts. We serve it over penne pasta with clumps of fresh wilted spinach on the side. It keeps well for several days in the refrigerator.

2 teaspoons olive oil
2 garlic cloves, minced
1 medium red onion, chopped (1½ cups)
1 cup white wine
2 cups heavy cream
¼ pound Gorgonzola cheese, crumbled
2 tablespoons Parmesan cheese, grated
¾ cup walnuts, toasted and chopped
1 tablespoon fresh basil, minced

Heat olive oil over low flame in an enamel saucepan. Sauté garlic and onions until soft, or about 5 minutes. Pour the wine into the pan, raise flame, and boil mixture for about 10 minutes, or until reduced to a syrup. Stir in the heavy cream, reduce flame, and simmer sauce about 10 minutes, or until it is reduced by almost half and lightly coats the back of a spoon. Strain the sauce through a fine sieve and return to the pan. Add cheeses, nuts, and basil, and stir over a low flame until cheese is completely melted. Add salt and pepper if you wish. *Yield: 1½ cups.*

Gruyère Cream Sauce

This simple cream sauce is a rich and aromatic cloak for hot pasta sprinkled with walnuts, or a platter of steamed spring vegetables. We also use it to nap a dish of baked fillet of sole, and to dress spinach-stuffed crepes. It keeps well in the refrigerator for up to a week.

1 shallot, minced
½ cup dry white wine
½ cup heavy cream
4 ounces Swiss Gruyère cheese, grated
dash of freshly ground nutmeg

In a small enameled saucepan, boil the shallots in the wine until liquid is reduced to a couple of syrupy tablespoons. Pour in the cream and heat to a vigorous simmer. Add the grated cheese and nutmeg and cook while stirring until the cheese is melted and the sauce is smooth and thick. Add salt and pepper if you wish. Cool to room temperature before storing. *Yield: ¾ cup.*

Orange Habanero Sauce

This clear, tangy sauce makes a simple baked or poached fish sit up and sing! If you wish your hot sauce to really flame, add more habanero chile. Best used on the same day you make it.

1¾ cups freshly squeezed orange juice
1½ tablespoons raw sugar
1 large, ripe habanero chile (orange or red), seeded
*   and minced*

Combine ingredients in a heavy enamel saucepan and bring to a boil over medium flame. Cook until reduced by half, about 10 minutes. Let the sauce cool, and then pour through a fine sieve. *Yield: About ¾ cup.*

Spiced Mango Coulis

A sweet fruit sauce for simple cakes or French toast, it's also delicious with grilled or baked fish. If you want it fiery, toss ½ teaspoon of minced fresh serrano chile into the sauce after it's made. Use immediately or chill for up to 2 days.

½ fresh mango, peeled and chopped (about ½ cup)
¼ cup spiced tea (see below)
1 tablespoon raw sugar

Combine ingredients in blender and puree. Force through a sieve. *Yield: About ¾ cup.*

(To make spiced tea, toss 4 whole peppercorns, a 1-inch piece of stick cinnamon, a generous teaspoon of minced fresh ginger and a teaspoon of black tea into 1½ cups of boiling water. Reduce flame to low and simmer for about 5 minutes. Turn off the flame and steep the tea for 15 minutes, then strain.)

Honeydew and Jalapeño Coulis

This fresh, piquant sauce has lovely color, bright flavor, and a touch of lingering heat. Use it to nap poached fish or seafood, or cold sliced ham. Use the sauce the same day you make it.

½ pound honeydew (about ¼ of a melon), cut up
1 pickled jalapeño chile, seeded
½ teaspoon fresh lime juice

Combine ingredients in a food processor and puree. Force through a fine sieve. Add salt and pepper if you wish. *Yield: About ¾ cup.*

Pink Peppercorn and Cherry Sauce

This sweet and fiery fruit sauce is a natural with cold roasted chicken, turkey, or duck. We also love it with poached fruit and crème anglaise. It's best used within a day or two after making it.

12 bing cherries, pitted
2 teaspoons lemon juice
¼ cup white wine or water
1 tablespoon raw sugar
¼ teaspoon pink peppercorns

Combine ingredients in a food processor and puree. Let stand for 20 minutes. Force the sauce through a fine sieve. *Yield: About ¾ cup.*

Ancho Apricot Coulis

Rich deep flavor and mild heat characterize this simple fruit and chile sauce, which takes to grilled chicken like a natural. We like it with fish, too. It's a great dressing for poached pears or chiles rellenos. It's best used the same day you make it.

2 apricots, pitted
¼ cup water
1 tablespoon white wine
1 teaspoon raw sugar
1 tablespoon ancho chile puree (see pages 178–79)

Combine ingredients in a food processor and puree. Force through a fine sieve. Add salt and pepper if you wish. *Yield: About ½ cup.*

Spiced Vanilla Pear Sauce

This fragrant sauce is a lovely accompaniment for pork, poached fruit, or simple cakes. It's best used immediately after you make it.

1 large, ripe Bartlett pear, cored and chopped
2 teaspoons lemon juice
½ cup spiced tea (see below)
1 tablespoon raw sugar
½ vanilla bean

Split the vanilla bean and scrape the seeds into the bowl of a food processor. (Reserve the bean for another use.) Add all remaining ingredients and puree. Force the sauce through a fine sieve. *Yield: About 1 cup.*

(To make spiced tea, toss 4 whole peppercorns, a 1-inch piece of stick cinnamon, a generous teaspoon of minced fresh ginger and a teaspoon of black tea into 1½ cups of boiling water. Reduce flame to low and simmer for about 5 minutes. Turn off the flame and steep the tea for 15 minutes, and then strain.)

Roasted Peach Pasilla Sauce

This sweet-hot, roasted fruit puree is delicious with pork or poultry, and makes a delightful and unusual dessert sauce over ice cream, poached pears, or simple cakes. It keeps in the refrigerator for up to a week, and also freezes beautifully.

4 tablespoons unsalted butter
4 tablespoons raw sugar
1 fresh orange, juiced
4 large peaches, skinned, pitted, and sliced
⅛ teaspoon ground cumin
1 tablespoon pasilla chile puree (see pages 178–79)

Preheat oven to 425 degrees F. In a heavy oven-proof skillet melt the butter, sugar, and orange juice together over medium flame, while stirring, for about 8 minutes, or until the sugar is dissolved. Turn off the flame, add sliced peaches and cumin to the skillet, and stir to coat peaches. Roast the peaches for 20 minutes, remove from the oven, and let stand 5 minutes. Scrape peaches into a food processor, add pasilla chile puree, and process to a smooth sauce. *Yield: About 2 cups.*

Dried Cherry Sauce

This simple sauce is irresistible over rich, dark chocolate cake or homemade ice cream. We always have it on hand during the holidays as an instant dessert for unexpected callers. It keeps well in the refrigerator for a week or more (unless you have teenagers at home!).

> *1½ cups dried sour cherries*
> *½ cup kirsch*
> *½ cup water*
> *1 cup cherry preserves*
> *1 cinnamon stick*
> *1 tablespoon fresh orange zest*

Combine ingredients in a small saucepan over medium flame. Cover and simmer for 5 minutes, stirring occasionally. Allow to cool completely at room temperature, and then chill. *Yield: About 2 cups.*

Dressings

Balsamic Basil Vinaigrette

This is a rich, aromatic dressing we like to use with any kind of greens and for drizzling over black olives, fresh sliced tomatoes, rings of sweet onion, sautéed mushrooms, steamed and chilled asparagus, or creamy artichoke hearts. It's best to use it up within a day or two after you make it.

> ¼ cup balsamic vinegar
> 1 cup virgin olive oil
> ¼ cup fresh basil leaves, minced

Whisk the oil into the vinegar by drops to make an emulsion. Stir in the fresh basil. Taste for seasoning and add salt and freshly ground black pepper if you wish. *Yield: 1 ½ cups.*

Hot Pepper Vinaigrette

This sweet tangy dressing with lingering heat is wonderful on Boston lettuce tossed with chopped scallions, nuts, and mandarin oranges. Use Tabasco or *Your Hot Pepper Sauce* (see page 42). It will keep in the refrigerator for a month.

¼ cup red wine vinegar
½ teaspoon liquid hot pepper sauce
2 tablespoons raw sugar
1 cup sunflower or canola oil

Whisk vinegar, pepper sauce, and sugar together until sugar dissolves. Add oil by drops and then in a thin stream to make an emulsion. Chill for an hour to develop flavors. Add salt and pepper if you wish. *Yield: 1 ¾ cups.*

Lemon Vinaigrette

We serve this tangy fresh dressing on Belgian endive with chopped hard-boiled egg, chopped walnuts, and crumbled Roquefort cheese. It's good over fresh fruit, too. It will keep refrigerated for up to a month.

2 garlic cloves, minced
1 tablespoon lemon zest, minced
¼ teaspoon salt
¼ cup fresh lemon juice
1 cup extra virgin olive oil
¼ teaspoon freshly ground black pepper
3 tablespoons fresh parsley leaves, minced

In a small mortar, crush the garlic and lemon zest with the salt to make a paste. Scrape the paste into a deep bowl and whisk in the lemon juice. Add the oil by drops and then in a thin stream to make an emulsion. Stir in the pepper and parsley and let stand for an hour. Add more pepper and salt if you wish. *Yield: About 1 ¼ cups.*

Chinese Cilantro Vinaigrette

This is not only a good salad dressing but also a delicious marinade for grilled or baked fish (reserve a bit of dressing to serve over the fish after it's cooked). The distinctive cilantro flavor stands up well in a cold corn and black bean salad, or a pasta salad with roasted poblano chile and red pepper strips. It will keep refrigerated for up to a week.

2 tablespoons fresh cilantro leaves, minced
2 tablespoons fresh ginger, minced
2 tablespoons fresh lime juice
¼ cup soy sauce
¼ cup rice vinegar
¾ cup sunflower oil

Whisk the ingredients together in a small bowl, adding oil by drops and then in a thin stream to make an emulsion. Let stand for an hour to meld flavors. Add salt and pepper if you wish. *Yield: 1½ cups.*

Oregano Vinaigrette

We serve this fresh herb dressing with bitter greens like radicchio or arugula, or to marinate steamed vegetables à la Grecque. It's also a good dressing for a cold pasta salad tossed with black olives, red onion, a little ripe goat cheese, and some chopped sun-dried tomatoes. It will keep refrigerated for one week.

3 tablespoons fresh oregano, chopped
3 tablespoons garlic, minced
¼ cup red wine vinegar
1 cup extra virgin olive oil

Whisk ingredients together, adding oil in a slow stream to make an emulsion. Add salt and pepper if you wish. *Yield: 1¼ cups.*

Sesame Soy Vinaigrette

We serve this zesty and rich-tasting dressing on fresh baby spinach with toasted croutons, sweet red onion, and mandarin oranges. Try it on any robust greens with fresh fruit and nuts, or in a salad of cooked beans or bulgur wheat. It will keep in the refrigerator for up to a month.

> *2 tablespoons fresh lemon juice*
> *4 tablespoons rice vinegar or champagne vinegar*
> *¼ cup soy sauce*
> *2 tablespoons sesame seeds, toasted and lightly crushed*
> *2 tablespoons sesame oil*
> *¼ cup peanut oil*

In a small bowl, whisk together the lemon juice, vinegar, soy sauce, and sesame seeds. Add the oils by drops and then in a thin stream to make an emulsion. Add salt and pepper if you wish. *Yield: ¾ cup.*

Mustard Walnut Vinaigrette

This light dressing is a favorite with soft lettuces such as Boston Bibb or oak leaf. We like to top the dressed lettuces with toasted goat cheese and walnuts. The dressing keeps refrigerated for up to a month.

> *1 tablespoon prepared Dijon mustard*
> *1½ teaspoons shallots, minced*
> *¼ teaspoon salt*
> *½ teaspoon freshly ground black pepper*
> *¼ cup red wine vinegar*
> *1 cup walnut oil*

Whisk the ingredients together in a deep bowl, adding the oil by drops and then in a thin stream to make an emulsion. Let stand for an hour to meld flavors. Taste for seasoning and add more salt and pepper if you wish. *Yield: About 1¼ cups.*

Roasted Garlic Vinaigrette

For true garlic lovers, this thick vinaigrette packs a lot of punch. We like to serve this over baby spinach with sautéed portobello mushrooms, roasted red bell peppers, and crumbled feta cheese. It's also great with cold seafood salads, or as a dip for chilled fresh vegetables. It keeps well for several days in the refrigerator.

1 large head fresh garlic
¼ cup red wine vinegar
1 cup extra virgin olive oil

Preheat the oven to 400 degrees F. Separate the garlic cloves and wrap them tightly in aluminum foil. Roast the garlic until tender (35 to 40 minutes), and then cool. When cool enough to handle, peel the garlic cloves and place them in the bowl of a food processor. Add the vinegar to the food processor and pulse to a smooth puree, and then add the oil in a thin stream until the dressing is emulsified and smooth. Add salt and pepper if you wish. *Yield: About 1¼ cups.*

Sun-Dried Tomato Vinaigrette

This rich, sweet dressing is wonderful on greens and doubles as a great marinade for steaks and chops. It keeps well in the refrigerator for several days.

¼ cup sun-dried tomatoes, chopped
1 garlic clove, chopped
1 tablespoon fresh basil leaves
¼ cup balsamic vinegar
1 cup extra virgin olive oil

Pulse tomato, garlic, basil, and vinegar in a food processor until smooth and well mixed. With the processor on, slowly drizzle olive oil into the dressing until it is smooth and thick. Add salt and pepper if you wish. *Yield: 1⅓ cups.*

Shallot Vinaigrette

This is a rich and potent vinaigrette that stands up well to other strong flavors. Use it on a salad of romaine and arugula with onions and croutons. We've been known to marinate a good rib-eye steak in this dressing for 30 minutes before grilling. It keeps well in the refrigerator for up to a week.

3 large shallots, minced
1 tablespoon prepared Dijon mustard
2 tablespoons red wine vinegar
2 tablespoons sherry vinegar
½ cup olive oil
½ cup canola oil

In a small bowl, whisk shallots and mustard together. Whisk in vinegars, and add oils by drops and then a thin stream to make an emulsion. Add salt and pepper if you wish. *Yield: About 1¼ cups.*

Miso Vinaigrette

Japanese red miso is a tart fermented soybean paste with an interesting flavor. It's mainly used as a base for soups, but makes a good dressing for pungent field greens tossed with scallions, water chestnuts, and julienned pork or beef. It keeps well in the refrigerator for several days.

> *2 tablespoons red miso*
> *2 teaspoons prepared Dijon mustard*
> *1 tablespoon water*
> *1½ tablespoons fresh lemon juice*
> *¼ cup safflower oil*
> *1 teaspoon fresh ginger, minced*
> *1 scallion, minced*

In a bowl, mash together the miso, mustard, water, and lemon juice. Add the oil in a thin stream to make an emulsion, and then stir in the ginger and scallion. Chill for an hour to develop flavors. Add salt and pepper if you wish. *Yield: ½ cup.*

SAVORY MAYONNAISE DRESSINGS—Simply Grand!

Nothing could be simpler for turning cold roasted meats, poached seafood, or grilled vegetables into elegant dinner party fare. These flavorful dressings can be made in minutes and used in myriad ways, from napping chilled vegetables to jazzing up a brown-bag sandwich. Any good mayonnaise sauce can be lightened and filled out by stirring in a few tablespoons of sour cream, yogurt, or whipped cream.

We start with our own mayonnaise. It's simple to make and always has the distinctive flavor of our own fresh ingredients. We think it's a vast improvement over the sugary, homogenized products we can buy at the grocery store, which tend to reduce all mayonnaise dressings to the same "processed" flavor.

The oil you use is key to the flavor of your mayonnaise. We generally use safflower oil, which is neutral and delicate. For specific mayonnaise sauces we may use a combination of oils for flavor, including extra virgin olive oil. Try using different oils until you find your favorite combinations (see pages 172–74). If you can, buy locally produced fresh eggs; they will make a flavor difference as well. Fresh mayonnaise sauces should be used quickly; they can be kept refrigerated for up to a week.

Basic Mayonnaise

2 egg yolks
¼ teaspoon salt
2 teaspoons fresh lemon juice
1 cup oil

Start with everything at room temperature. Whirl the egg yolks, salt, and lemon juice in a food processor for 10 seconds (or whisk vigorously). Add the oil by drops until the mixture begins to thicken, and then add it by spoons while continuing to process or whisk until the mayonnaise is smooth and thick. Taste for seasoning and add more salt and white pepper (or more lemon juice, herbs, etc.) if you wish. *Yield: About 1 cup.*

Herb Mayonnaise Dressing

Herb mayonnaise is the perfect choice for dressing cold poached fish or cold roasted chicken. Good herb choices are peppery watercress, dill, tarragon, basil, cilantro, or rosemary. For a pleasant mix, use equal parts parsley, oregano, and chervil. Use within a day or two of whipping together.

> *1 cup Basic Mayonnaise (see page 67) or*
> *   purchased mayonnaise*
> *⅔ cup fresh herbs, minced*
> *1 teaspoon lemon juice*

Whisk the herbs and lemon juice into the mayonnaise and chill for an hour to develop flavors. Thin with cream or drops of white wine to desired consistency. Add salt and pepper if you wish. *Yield: About 1 cup.*

Pepper and Mint Mayonnaise Dressing

This rich, aromatic spread was made for cucumber sandwiches, and it's a great dressing for cold chicken, lamb, or pork. Use it within a day or two of whipping together.

> *1 cup Basic Mayonnaise (see page 67) or*
> *   purchased mayonnaise*
> *1 teaspoon champagne vinegar*
> *½ cup fresh mint leaves, minced*
> *⅛ teaspoon freshly-cracked black pepper*

Whisk ingredients together and chill for about an hour to develop flavors. Thin with drops of white wine to desired consistency. Taste for seasoning and add salt if you wish. *Yield: About 1 cup.*

Cilantro and Jalapeño Mayonnaise Dressing

We love this dressing for shrimp or lobster salad, and it is a zesty sandwich spread. Use it within a few days of mixing up.

> 1 cup Basic Mayonnaise (see page 67) or
>   purchased mayonnaise
> 1 pickled jalapeño chile, seeded and minced
> 2 tablespoons fresh cilantro leaves, minced
> ½ teaspoon lemon juice

Whisk ingredients together and chill for an hour to meld flavors. Thin with drops of white wine to desired consistency. Add salt and pepper if you wish. *Yield: About 1 cup.*

Chipotle Mayonnaise Dressing

This simple cold chile dressing is excellent for cold seafood or crabcakes, and adds great spark to a platter of steamed chilled vegetables. Use it within a few hours—the longer it sits, the hotter it will get! If it gets too fiery, cool it down with several tablespoons of sour cream.

> 1 cup Basic Mayonnaise (see page 67) or
>   purchased mayonnaise
> 1 teaspoon chipotle en adobo, minced (or to taste)

Whisk chipotle into mayonnaise and chill for an hour. Thin with drops of white wine to desired consistency. Add salt and pepper if you wish. *Yield: About 1 cup.*

Curried Mayonnaise Dressing

We think this one is marvelous for chicken salad and for dressing cold fresh fruit. Use it within a day or two of whipping it up.

1 cup Basic Mayonnaise (see page 67) or
*   purchased mayonnaise*
2 teaspoons curry powder
¼ teaspoon crushed garlic
1½ tablespoons roasted peanuts, finely chopped

Whisk ingredients together and chill for an hour. Thin with drops of white wine to desired consistency. Add salt and pepper if you wish. *Yield: About 1 cup.*

Spiced Mayonnaise Dressing

This is another good dressing for cold chicken. It goes well with cold beef or pork, too. Use it within a few days of mixing it up.

1 cup Basic Mayonnaise (see page 67) or
*   purchased mayonnaise*
⅓ cup thick mango chutney, pureed
1 tablespoon shredded coconut, toasted

Whisk ingredients together and chill for an hour. Thin with drops of white wine to desired consistency. Add salt and pepper if you wish. *Yield: About 1⅓ cups.*

Red Chile Rémoulade Dressing

We love this classic dressing with cold shrimp or lobster, as a
dressing for steamed chilled asparagus, or tucked into hollowed
cherry tomatoes. Use it within a day or two of making it.

*1 cup Basic Mayonnaise (see page 67) or
    purchased mayonnaise
1 teaspoon lemon juice
1 cornichon (or small sour gherkin), minced
2 large pimiento-stuffed olives, minced
1 scallion (white part only), minced
2 anchovy fillets, minced
1 teaspoon capers, minced
⅛ teaspoon red chile powder
1 tablespoon fresh parsley, minced*

Whisk ingredients together and chill for an hour. Thin with
drops of white wine to desired consistency. Taste for seasoning
and add salt and pepper if you want. *Yield: About 1¼ cups.*

Tuna Caper Dressing

This is the dressing of choice for cold veal or pork tenderloin that has been marinated, simmered, and chilled in the Italian manner. It's also wonderful with steamed chilled vegetables; over chilled hard-boiled eggs; or as a sandwich spread. Use it within a few days of whipping it up.

> ½ cup Basic Mayonnaise (see page 67) or
>   purchased mayonnaise
> 6-ounce can water-packed tuna, well-drained
> 2 teaspoons fresh lemon juice
> 1 tablespoon capers
> 6 anchovy fillets
> 1 tablespoon fresh parsley leaves, minced
> 1 pinch cayenne pepper

Combine ingredients in a food processor and puree. Add light olive oil if sauce is too thick. Add salt and pepper if you wish. *Yield: About 1½ cups.*

Spicy Orange Ginger Dressing

This dressing is grand with cold chicken or turkey, and it makes an unusual sandwich spread. We also serve it with crabcakes or fried shrimp. Use it within a day or two of whipping it up.

> 1 cup Basic Mayonnaise (see page 67) or
>   purchased mayonnaise
> 1½ tablespoons fresh lime juice
> 2 tablespoons Grand Marnier or orange liqueur
> 1 tablespoon Worcestershire sauce
> 1 teaspoon soy sauce

1 teaspoon Asian chile sauce
1½ teaspoons fresh ginger, minced
1 teaspoon fresh orange zest
2 tablespoons fresh cilantro leaves, minced

Whisk ingredients together and chill for an hour. Add salt and pepper if you wish. *Yield: 1½ cups.*

Green Goddess Dressing

This popular anchovy dressing is not only great with green salads, but it is a marvelous accompaniment to cold roasted meats and cheeses. If you're an anchovy fan, don't hesitate to use more fillets in the dressing (Kathleen has been known to use 5 or 6 in hers). For the freshest flavor, use the dressing within 24 hours.

1 tablespoon white wine vinegar
1 teaspoon fresh lemon juice
½ cup sour cream
½ cup Basic Mayonnaise (see page 67) or
    purchased mayonnaise
½ cup parsley, finely minced
1½ tablespoons fresh tarragon, finely minced
4 chives, finely minced
1 garlic clove, crushed and finely minced
2 anchovies (or more), finely minced

Whisk the vinegar and lemon juice into the sour cream, and then whisk the sour cream into the mayonnaise until smooth and well combined. Stir the minced herbs, garlic, and anchovies into the dressing and chill for an hour to develop flavors. Add salt and pepper if you wish. If dressing is too thick, thin out with spoons of milk. *Yield: 1½ cups.*

Peppery Avocado Dressing

This cool and savory dressing stands up well to the strong flavors of fresh arugula, watercress, and other pungent greens. We also love it as a dip for fresh vegetables, or as a sauce for grilled lamb kabobs or hot beef tacos. It will discolor eventually, so serve it within a couple of hours of assembling.

> 1 ripe Haas avocado
> 2 teaspoons fresh lime juice
> ½ cup Basic Mayonnaise (see page 67) or
>   purchased mayonnaise
> ½ fresh serrano chile, seeded and finely minced
> 1 tablespoon white onion, finely minced
> ½ tablespoon fresh cilantro leaves, finely minced
> ¼ teaspoon freshly ground black pepper

Peel the avocado, slice it quickly into the bowl of a food processor, and sprinkle with lime juice. Add remaining ingredients and pulse until well mixed. Puree the dressing until very smooth, adding a few more drops of lime juice if necessary for consistency. Chill the dressing for an hour to meld flavors. Add salt and more pepper if you wish. *Yield: 1 ½ cups.*

Spicy Thousand Island Dressing

This dressing is often a favorite with children, but it also has plenty of sweet-hot tang for the adult palate. It's great on a burger or a taco salad or for dressing chilled shrimp. It keeps well in the refrigerator for up to a week.

> *1 cup Basic Mayonnaise (see page 67) or*
>   *purchased mayonnaise*
> *½ cup ketchup*
> *¼ cup sweet pickle relish*
> *1 tablespoon sweet onion, minced*
> *1 teaspoon fresh garlic, minced*
> *dash or two of Your Hot Pepper Sauce (see page 42)*

Whisk ingredients together in a small bowl and chill for an hour to develop flavors. Add salt and pepper if you wish. *Yield: 1¾ cups.*

Chipotle Orange Marmalade Dressing

This is an easy and delicious spread for smoked turkey, honey-cured ham, or cheese sandwiches. It's great on cold roasted pork and on fresh fruit salad as well. It stays fresh for up to a week in the refrigerator, but you'll have trouble keeping it on hand!

> *½ cup Basic Mayonnaise (see page 67) or*
>   *purchased mayonnaise*
> *2 tablespoons chipotle chiles en adobo, minced*
> *3 tablespoons tart orange marmalade*

Whisk ingredients together. Add salt and pepper if you wish. *Yield: ¾ cup.*

Creamy Chive Dressing

This simple dressing is a delicious standby for any Cobb salad, chef's salad, or other composition of robust greens and chopped vegetables. Try it in fresh chicken or turkey salad. We also like it over hot baked potatoes or drizzled on potato pancakes or crispy corned beef hash. You can keep it refrigerated for up to a week.

½ cup sour cream
¼ cup Basic Mayonnaise (see page 67) or
*   purchased mayonnaise*
2 tablespoons buttermilk or whole milk
1 teaspoon apple cider vinegar
½ teaspoon fresh lemon juice
¼ teaspoon salt
dash of cayenne pepper or Your Hot Pepper Sauce
*   (see page 42)*
3 tablespoons fresh chives, chopped

In a medium bowl, whisk together all ingredients except chives until smooth and well blended. Stir in chives, taste for seasoning, and add more salt and pepper if you wish. *Yield: 2 cups.*

Raita

This smooth and creamy dressing from the Mediterranean is a perfect complement to grilled meats and vegetables, and a savory dip for pita toasts or crisp fresh vegetables. We also like a dollop in a bowl of hot, spicy soup. It keeps well in the refrigerator for a week or more.

2 cups plain yogurt
2 garlic cloves, chopped
1 tablespoon cumin seeds
1 tablespoon coriander seeds
1 tablespoon mustard seeds
1 tablespoon fresh cilantro leaves, chopped
1 tablespoon fresh ginger, minced
2 tablespoons fresh lime juice
1 teaspoon fresh lime zest

Set the yogurt in a fine sieve to drain for about 15 minutes. Toast and lightly crush the seeds. Combine drained yogurt with seeds and remaining ingredients in a food processor and puree. Add salt and pepper if you wish. *Yield: 2 cups.*

Cumin Sour Cream Dressing

Like raita, this refreshing sauce has a Mediterranean touch, and it is especially good with grilled lamb chops and vegetable kabobs. We also think it's a delightful side dressing for tacos, quesadillas, and enchiladas. It keeps well in the refrigerator for up to a week.

1 cup sour cream
1 tablespoon milk
½ tablespoon cumin seed, toasted and crushed
1 tablespoon red bell pepper, finely minced
1 scallion, minced
2 teaspoons fresh mint leaves, minced
1 teaspoon fresh lime juice

Whisk ingredients together and chill for an hour. Add salt and pepper if you wish. *Yield: About 1 cup.*

Sour Cream Horseradish Dressing

A standing roast of beef cries out for a creamy horseradish sauce like this one, but this sauce is also very versatile. Use it to nap tender-crisp green beans, asparagus, or carrots; stir it into potato, mushroom, or black bean soup; ladle it over roasted beets and turnips, or serve it with a platter of cold meats and cheeses. It keeps well in the refrigerator for up to a week.

1 cup sour cream
1 tablespoon milk
2 tablespoons fresh horseradish, grated
1 teaspoon lemon juice
1 tablespoon fresh chives, minced

Whisk ingredients together and chill for an hour. Taste for seasoning and add salt and white pepper if you wish. *Yield: About 1 cup.*

Spicy Sour Cream Mustard Dressing

The traditional accompaniment for hot corned beef and cabbage, this well-flavored dressing is also very good with poached salmon, hot crabcakes, cold shrimp or lobster, baked ham, and steamed green vegetables. It keeps well in the refrigerator for up to a week.

1 cup sour cream
1 tablespoon milk
3 tablespoons prepared Dijon or hot mustard
1 teaspoon fresh lemon juice
1 tablespoon fresh parsley, minced

Whisk ingredients together and chill for an hour. Taste for seasoning and add salt and white pepper if you wish. *Yield: About 1 cup.*

Lemon Yogurt Dressing

This lemony sweet dressing turns a fresh fruit salad into a healthy summer luncheon that's like a taste of ambrosia. It keeps well in the refrigerator for up to a week.

¼ teaspoon freshly grated lemon zest
2 teaspoons fresh lemon juice
1½ tablespoons honey
½ cup light cream
¼ cup plain yogurt
¼ teaspoon vanilla
1 pinch salt

Whisk ingredients together in a bowl and chill for an hour to develop flavors. Taste for seasoning and add more salt or a few drops of lemon juice if you wish. *Yield: About ¾ cup.*

Stilton Cream Dressing

This is one of Audrey's special dressings for family Christmas Eve dinner. She serves it over tossed green salad with herbed croutons, but we also think it's a wonderful spread for cold roast beef sandwiches. Try it as a rich dip for fresh vegetables, or for wedges of crispy apples or mellow pears. If you can't find Stilton, substitute Roquefort. It keeps well for several days in the refrigerator.

> *1 egg*
> *1 teaspoon raw sugar*
> *¼ cup apple cider vinegar*
> *¼ cup dry sherry*
> *1 cup olive oil*
> *1 cup canola oil*
> *4 ounces Stilton cheese, crumbled*
> *1 garlic clove, lightly crushed*

With a whisk (or in a food processor) beat the egg until pale yellow. Still whisking, sprinkle in the sugar, and then add vinegar and sherry slowly and whisk until thick. Add the oils by drops and then in a thin stream to make a thick emulsion. Pour the dressing into a deep bowl and stir in the Stilton. Skewer the garlic on a toothpick and sink it into the dressing; chill for an hour or two. Before serving, bring the dressing to room temperature and remove and discard the garlic. Add salt and pepper if you wish. *Yield: 3 cups.*

Creamy Gorgonzola Dressing

This very rich blue cheese dressing makes an instant luncheon or supper dish out of fresh baby greens and tomatoes. Serve the salad with crusty French bread and a glass of red wine and no one will leave the table hungry! The dressing will keep refrigerated for a week.

⅓ cup heavy cream
1 tablespoon fresh tarragon
1½ tablespoons white wine vinegar
6 ounces Gorgonzola or other blue-veined cheese
¼ cup milk
¼ cup Basic Mayonnaise (see page 67) or
    purchased mayonnaise
1 tablespoon grainy prepared mustard

Pulse ingredients together in a food processor until well mixed. Add salt and pepper if you wish. *Yield: About 1½ cups.*

Feta Cheese Dressing

We like this dressing on fresh greens right from the farmers' market, served with grilled fish or lamb chops. It's also good for dunking fresh vegetables, or drizzling over a pizza or fresh spinach quiche. It will keep refrigerated for up to a week, so it's a great one to have on hand.

¼ cup milk
⅓ cup light cream
1½ tablespoons white wine vinegar
¼ cup Basic Mayonnaise (see page 67) or
    purchased mayonnaise
1½ tablespoons fresh basil, minced
6 ounces feta cheese, crumbled fine

In a small bowl, whisk the milk, cream, and vinegar into the mayonnaise until smooth. Stir in the basil and the feta cheese, and chill for an hour. Add salt and pepper if you wish. *Yield: About 1 cup.*

Warm Citrus Dressing

We love this dressing over fresh spinach leaves tossed with red onion rings, sliced oranges, and Gruyère croutons. It's also great with steamed fresh asparagus or sugar snap peas, or over a fresh fruit salad. It keeps several days in the refrigerator.

4 tablespoons frozen orange juice concentrate, thawed
1 tablespoon fresh lemon juice
3 tablespoons honey
½ cup water
½ tablespoon fresh ginger, chopped
1 garlic clove, chopped
⅔ cup canola oil

In a food processor, puree all ingredients except the oil until well mixed. Refrigerate the mixture for at least 1 hour and up to 3 hours. Pour the mixture into a small saucepan and heat while stirring over a gentle flame until warm but not hot. Whisk the oil into the dressing by drops and then in a slow stream to make an emulsion. Add salt and pepper if you wish. Serve the dressing warm or at room temperature. *Yield: About 1 cup.*

Poppy Seed Dressing

We discovered this wonderful sweet dressing accompanying a bowl of sparkling fresh fruit on an Easter buffet. It keeps well for up to a week in the refrigerator.

1 cup raw sugar
¼ cup white wine vinegar
¼ cup poppy seeds
1 teaspoon dry mustard
1 cup safflower or canola oil

Stir the sugar into the vinegar until it is dissolved, and then pour into the bowl of a food processor. Add the poppy seeds and mustard and process into a smooth paste. With the motor running, add oil in droplets and then a thin stream to make an emulsion. Add salt and pepper if you wish. *Yield: About 1½ cups.*

Tahini Dressing

Tahini (a paste of sesame seeds) has been used as a staple flavoring in the Mediterranean for thousands of years, but it is still a delightful change of pace for most of us. It keeps for months under refrigeration, so it's a good item to have on hand. This dressing is good for any mixed green salad and is also a delicious side dressing for curry dishes or shish kabobs. Refrigerated, it keeps for several days.

> *½ teaspoon cumin seeds, toasted*
> *½ teaspoon coriander seeds, toasted*
> *¼ cup tahini (available bottled in most groceries)*
> *¼ cup hot water*
> *2 teaspoons white wine vinegar*
> *½ cup plain yogurt*

In a small mortar, grind the seeds fine. In a bowl, whisk the tahini with hot water until smooth, and then whisk in the seeds, vinegar, and yogurt. Refrigerate for an hour to develop flavors. Add salt and pepper if you wish. *Yield: 1 cup.*

Roasted Pepper Aioli

This rich and robust dressing, powered by garlic and roasted red pepper, is magnificent with baked, broiled, or sautéed fish and makes a fine accompaniment for crisp-tender fresh vegetables. Stir it into a fish or chicken soup, or serve it on the side for dipping crusty French bread. It keeps for several days in the refrigerator.

> *1 cup virgin olive oil*
> *1 large head garlic, cloves peeled and roughly chopped*
> *1 red bell pepper, roasted, peeled, seeded, and chopped*
>   *(see pages 176–77)*
> *¼ cup fresh parsley leaves, minced*
> *1 French baguette (or 5 thick slices of French bread),*
>   *crust removed*
> *⅓ cup red wine vinegar*
> *1 tablespoon fresh lemon juice*
> *2 or 3 tablespoons water*

Pour the olive oil into a deep glass or ceramic bowl. Crush the chopped garlic into the oil with the back of a wooden spoon. Stir the pepper and parsley into the oil, and then tear the bread into chunks and thoroughly stir the chunks into the oil. Let the mixture stand for about an hour, stirring up occasionally, until the bread is thoroughly softened. Pour the mixture into a food processor and pulse until it is a thick, fluffy puree. Toss in remaining ingredients and continue to process to the consistency you like; add more water if the sauce is too thick. Add salt and pepper if you wish. *Yield: 2 cups.*

Marinades, Glazes & Rubs

Soy Wasabi Paste

This pungent rub is made for fresh tuna steaks, but it is strong enough to work well for any cut of beef or pork you plan to grill. Marinate for several hours or overnight, and then wipe off the rub before grilling the meat.

1 teaspoon honey
2 teaspoons sherry
1 tablespoon soy sauce
1 tablespoon water
2 tablespoons wasabi powder
½ tablespoon fresh ginger, grated

Stir the honey, sherry, soy sauce, and water together until the honey is dissolved. Stir the liquid mixture into the wasabi powder to make a thick paste, adding more water if necessary. Stir the grated ginger into the paste. *Yield: ¼ cup paste, enough for 2 steaks or chops.*

Thai Curry Marinade

This pungent marinade is especially good for pork, but it also does wonders for chicken. If you cannot locate Thai red curry paste, substitute a tablespoon of your favorite curry powder mixed into 5 tablespoons of ancho or pasilla chile puree (see pages 178–79). The marinade keeps well for several days in the refrigerator. Always discard the marinade once it has been used.

½ cup molasses
½ cup soy sauce
¼ cup Thai red curry paste
2 large cloves garlic, crushed
1 tablespoon fresh ginger, minced
2 tablespoons fresh cilantro leaves, chopped

In a small bowl, stir the molasses into the soy sauce until it is dissolved. Whisk in the remaining ingredients. When you are ready to marinate, pour the marinade into a heavy plastic freezer bag, add the meat, seal the bag, and refrigerate the marinating meat at least an hour and up to 5 hours. *Yield: 1¼ cups marinade.*

Savory Herb Marinade

This red wine marinade is strong enough to impart great flavor to beef, lamb, or pork. Marinate the meat for several hours before grilling, if you can, and use the marinade to baste meat while it's cooking.

½ cup dry red wine
2 tablespoons fresh lemon juice
¾ cup olive oil
2 shallots, minced
2 tablespoons fresh parsley leaves, minced

2 tablespoons fresh oregano, minced
2 tablespoons fresh chervil, minced
¼ teaspoon freshly ground black pepper

Stir wine and lemon juice together. Whisk in the oil by drops and then a thin stream to make an emulsion. Stir in remaining ingredients. Taste for seasoning and add salt if you wish. *Yield: About 1¾ cups.*

Balsamic Herb Marinade

This is a rich, aromatic marinade that's especially good for fish or chicken. If possible, marinate meat for several hours and up to 24 hours before grilling. Reserve some to use as a baste for meat and vegetables on the grill.

¼ cup balsamic vinegar
1 teaspoon prepared Dijon mustard
¾ cup virgin olive oil
¼ cup fresh basil leaves, minced
2 tablespoons fresh parsley leaves, minced
¼ teaspoon freshly ground black pepper

Whisk the vinegar and mustard together, and then whisk the oil into the vinegar by drops to make an emulsion. Stir in the fresh herbs and pepper. Taste for seasoning and add salt if you wish. *Yield: 1¼ cups.*

Tomato Garlic Marinade

This marinade is especially good for lamb or for strongly flavored fish steaks. Marinate the meat for several hours if you can, and use the marinade to baste while grilling. It's great for vegetables, too.

½ cup tomato juice or V-8 Juice
3 tablespoons fresh lemon juice
2 tablespoons white wine
2 teaspoons dried rosemary, crushed
1 teaspoon dried thyme, crushed
¼ teaspoon freshly ground pepper
½ cup extra virgin olive oil
2 large garlic cloves, crushed and chopped
2 tablespoons fresh parsley leaves, minced

Whisk together the tomato juice, lemon juice, wine, and dried herbs. Whisk in the oil by drops and then in a thin stream to make an emulsion. Stir in the garlic and fresh parsley. Taste for seasoning and add salt if you wish. *Yield: About 1¾ cups.*

Dijon Mustard Marinade

This robust marinade is good for beef, lamb, or chicken, and it also works well for fillets of salmon or white-fleshed fish. Marinate the meat for several hours or overnight.

3 tablespoons prepared Dijon mustard
¼ cup red wine vinegar
½ cup virgin olive oil
1 shallot, minced
2 large garlic cloves, crushed and chopped
½ teaspoon freshly ground black pepper

Whisk mustard and vinegar together in a deep bowl. Add the oil by drops and then in the thin stream to make an emulsion. Stir in the shallot, garlic, and pepper. Taste for seasoning and add more salt if you wish. *Yield: About ¾ cup.*

Teriyaki Marinade

We think that it's hard to improve on this longtime favorite marinade for beef steaks. Marinate the meat for several hours or overnight before putting it on the grill. This marinade also works well for chicken and is great on almost any grilled vegetables.

> *5 tablespoons honey*
> *½ cup soy sauce*
> *2 tablespoons dry sherry*
> *1 tablespoon rice vinegar*
> *⅓ cup peanut oil*
> *1 tablespoon fresh ginger, grated*

In a small bowl, whisk honey, soy sauce, sherry, and vinegar together. Add the oil by drops and then in a thin stream to make an emulsion. Stir in the ginger. Taste for seasoning and add cracked pepper if you wish. *Yield: ¾ cup.*

Sweet Mint Marinade

This sweet fresh marinade is made for lamb chops, but works really well with chicken and with some grilled vegetables, including leeks, scallions, and onions. Marinate the meat for several hours before grilling, if you can, and use the marinade to baste meat while it's cooking.

> *½ cup white wine*
> *1 tablespoon white wine vinegar*
> *2 tablespoons honey*
> *¼ cup olive oil*
> *1 shallot, minced*
> *3 tablespoons fresh mint leaves, minced*
> *¼ teaspoon freshly ground black pepper*

In a small saucepan, stir wine, vinegar, and honey together until honey melts. Whisk in the oil by drops and then in a thin stream to make an emulsion. Stir in remaining ingredients. Taste for seasoning and add salt if you wish. *Yield: About 1¾ cups.*

Red Chile Honey Glaze

We use this glaze for chicken and for fillets of any mild white-fleshed fish (orange roughy, monkfish, grouper, etc.), whether we're grilling, broiling, or baking. If you're using it on the grill, remember that it has a high sugar content, so don't start basting the meat until it is within 5 to 10 minutes of being done. Because it keeps in the refrigerator almost indefinitely, this glaze is a good one to have on hand.

> *1 cup honey*
> *¼ cup red chile powder (medium hot is best)*
> *1 scant teaspoon salt*
> *1 teaspoon freshly ground black pepper*

Warm the honey over a gentle flame to medium hot (do not scorch it!) and stir in the chile, salt, and pepper until smooth and fully incorporated into the honey. Cool the honey and store in a glass jar in the refrigerator. Rewarm the honey before using to baste grilled, broiled, or baked fish or poultry. *Yield: 1 cup.*

Orange Ginger Grilling Glaze

We love this sweet-hot glaze for chicken or pork chops done on the grill. Use it as a mop during the last 10 or 15 minutes on the grill, or to baste grilled shrimp just as they come off the fire.

¼ cup orange marmalade
⅓ cup apple cider or white wine
1 tablespoon Worcestershire sauce
1 tablespoon fresh ginger, grated

Mix ingredients together in a small enameled saucepan and bring to the simmer over medium flame. Stir until well combined, and then cool. Add salt and pepper if you wish. *Yield: About ¾ cup.*

Hot Whiskey Grill Glaze

This is one of our favorite glazes for adding pungent hot barbecue flavor to red meats and chicken, either on the grill or in the oven. We also use it for simmering browned meatballs into knock-out appetizer bites. It's simple to make and keeps well in the refrigerator for weeks.

> *½ cup of bourbon whiskey*
> *½ cup ketchup*
> *2 tablespoons ancho or pasilla chile puree (see pages 178–79)*
> *¼ cup dark molasses*
> *¼ cup soy sauce*
> *¼ cup olive oil*
> *2 teaspoons Your Hot Pepper Sauce (see page 42)*

Whisk ingredients together in a heavy saucepan and simmer over moderate flame about 5 minutes. Taste for seasoning and add salt and pepper or more hot pepper sauce if you wish. Cool the glaze to room temperature. Brush steaks, chops, or chickens with glaze only during the last 15 minutes on a grill; if you brush earlier, the glaze could burn. For oven-finished barbecue, put browned meat in a roasting pan, coat with glaze, and bake at about 350 degrees F until done. *Yield: About 1½ cups.*

The Basic Dry Rub

You can make a dry marinade of virtually any combination of ground spices and dried herbs that you love by experimenting to find the best combinations. If you make a lot at one time, store your mix exactly the way you would any dried herb or ground spice—in an airtight container away from heat and light—and it will keep for up to a year. We don't have the space for that kind of storage, so we just mix our rubs when we need them.

We usually bind rubs together before using with lots of crushed garlic, or with olive oil to make a paste. The object is to impart a distinctive flavor to meat before it goes on the grill, so rub the mix into the meat well, and let it "marinate" several hours or overnight. We always wipe the rub off the meat before cooking if we're going to grill, broil, or pan-sear to avoid burning the spices.

Appearing below are some dry rubs on the basis of which you can build your own. Try different chile powders and different herbs in different proportions. Turn them into pastes with crushed fresh garlic, wine or brandy, sherry vinegar, soy sauce, or yogurt. . . . The sky is the limit!

Chile Rub

1 tablespoon red chile powder
1 tablespoon pasilla or ancho chile powder
1 tablespoon cumin powder
1 teaspoon dried oregano
¼ teaspoon cinnamon powder

Curry Rub

2 tablespoons curry powder
1 tablespoon cumin powder
½ tablespoon sweet paprika
¼ teaspoon clove powder
¼ teaspoon red jalapeño powder

Dill Rub

2 tablespoons dried dill, rubbed
1 tablespoon raw sugar
1 teaspoon mustard seed, lightly crushed
⅛ teaspoon cracked pepper

Rosemary Rub

2 tablespoons dried rosemary, rubbed
2 teaspoons dried parsley, rubbed
1 teaspoon dried thyme, rubbed
⅛ teaspoon cracked pepper

Ginger Wasabi Rub

1 tablespoon ginger powder
1 tablespoon wasabi powder
1 tablespoon raw sugar
1 teaspoon mustard seed, crushed
½ teaspoon coriander seeds, crushed

Chipotle Chile Rub

This chile paste rub is fiery hot with the rich smoky flavor of chipotle chiles. Use it to marinate meats or fish steaks (several hours or overnight), and then wipe off the rub before grilling. This moist rub also adds a great kick to salad dressings, sauces, soups, and stews. The rub will keep for several weeks in the refrigerator.

3 dried chipotle chiles
1 teaspoon raw sugar
1½ teaspoons white wine vinegar
2 teaspoons white onion, minced
2 fresh garlic cloves, minced
1 teaspoon dried oregano, crushed
2 teaspoons cumin seed, toasted and crushed
1 scant teaspoon salt
1 tablespoon canola oil (or less)

Rinse the chiles, remove stems and seeds, and cover with ¾ cup of boiling water. Let the chiles soak for 15 to 20 minutes, or until soft. Meanwhile, stir the sugar into the vinegar to dissolve. Remove the chiles (reserving the soaking liquid), tear them into pieces, and put them in a food processor with 2 tablespoons of their soaking liquid. Add sugar and vinegar and remaining ingredients and pulse to a thick puree, adding more chile-soaking liquid by the teaspoon as necessary. Scrape the marinade into a clean, dry glass jar, and cover the surface with a film of canola oil. Cover the jar tightly and store in the refrigerator until needed. *Yield: About ⅓ cup.*

Red Chile Brandy Rub

Full of hearty red chile flavor, this simple rub is a superb
marinade for wild game, and just as good for domestic duck or
turkey or a thick pot roast. Marinate the meat in a coating of
rub for up to 24 hours, and then braise, pot roast, or clay bake in
a slow oven for several hours. A jar of rub keeps well in the
refrigerator for up to a week.

½ tablespoon raw sugar
2 tablespoons Marsala or brandy
2 or 3 large garlic cloves, crushed with a teaspoon of salt
2 tablespoons red chile powder
2 tablespoons virgin olive oil (or less)

Dissolve the sugar in the brandy, and then crush all ingredients
together until well mixed. Add olive oil by drops until you have
the consistency you want. Scrape the rub into a small glass jar,
float a coating of olive oil over the top and refrigerate until ready
to use. *Yield: About ⅓ cup.*

 # Slaws

Jalapeño Slaw

This feisty slaw has great color and a hot kick! We love it with anything hot off the barbecue grill. It keeps well in the refrigerator for several days.

Slaw

¼ head white cabbage, shredded (2 cups)
⅓ head red cabbage, shredded (1 cup)
2 carrots, shredded (¾ cup)
1 small red bell pepper, julienned (½ cup)
1 small yellow bell pepper, julienned (½ cup)
½ small red onion, thinly sliced (½ cup)

Dressing

1 cup Basic Mayonnaise (see page 67) or
     purchased mayonnaise
3 tablespoons white wine vinegar
1 tablespoon honey
2 pickled jalapeño chiles, seeded and minced
1 teaspoon juice from pickled chiles
¼ teaspoon salt

Combine vegetables in a large salad bowl. Whisk dressing ingredients until smooth and creamy, and then pour dressing over the slaw and toss. Add pepper and more salt if you wish. *Yield: 4 to 5 cups.*

Harlequin Vegetable Slaw

This colorful salad makes a good topping for your favorite
burgers or a beautiful accompaniment for a fresh salmon fillet. It
keeps well in the refrigerator for several days.

Slaw

½ head Napa cabbage, shredded (4 cups)
½ red bell pepper, thinly julienned (½ cup)
½ yellow bell pepper, thinly julienned (½ cup)
1 medium cucumber, peeled and thinly julienned (1 cup)
4 scallions, thinly sliced on the diagonal

Dressing

⅓ cup Basic Mayonnaise (see page 67) or
    purchased mayonnaise
⅓ cup sour cream
2 tablespoons apple cider vinegar
¼ teaspoon salt
⅛ teaspoon freshly ground black pepper

Toss vegetables together in a large bowl. Whisk dressing
ingredients together until smooth and creamy, pour over the
slaw and mix well. Add pepper and more salt if you wish. *Yield:
5 cups.*

Creamy Garlic Slaw

This creamy, flavorful slaw is great for a picnic or a backyard barbecue, and we love lots of it with hot fried chicken. It keeps well in the refrigerator for several days.

Slaw

½ head white cabbage, shredded (4 cups)
½ tablespoon raw sugar
½ tablespoon salt
3 medium carrots, shredded (1 cup)
2 tablespoons green bell pepper, finely diced
1 shallot, minced

Dressing

¼ cup Basic Mayonnaise (see page 67) or
    purchased mayonnaise
¼ cup sour cream
½ tablespoon fresh lemon juice
½ teaspoon fresh lemon zest
1 large garlic clove, minced
¼ teaspoon freshly ground black pepper
½ teaspoon caraway seeds

Shred cabbage into a large glass bowl, sprinkle with sugar and salt, cover with cold water, and refrigerate 2 to 3 hours. In a large salad bowl, whisk dressing ingredients together until smooth. Stir the carrots, bell pepper, and shallots into the dressing. Drain the shredded cabbage well, and then toss with the dressing. Add pepper and more salt if you wish. *Yield: 4 cups.*

Fennel and Apple Slaw

This is a delicious winter slaw to accompany any roasted meat, or to make a meal served with a homemade soup and crusty fresh bread. It keeps well in the refrigerator for a day or two.

Slaw

½ medium red onion, finely chopped (½ cup)
1 large green apple, diced (about 1 cup)
1 large red apple, diced (about 1 cup)
1 fennel bulb, diced (about 1 cup)
½ cup Honey Roasted Walnuts, roughly chopped
    (see page 183)
¼ head white cabbage, shredded (about 2 cups)

Dressing

½ cup Basic Mayonnaise (see page 67) or
    purchased mayonnaise
1 tablespoon walnut oil
1 tablespoon white wine vinegar
1 teaspoon lemon juice
1 teaspoon fennel seeds, crushed
1 tablespoon honey
1 pinch salt
1 pinch freshly ground black pepper

Whisk dressing ingredients together until smooth and set aside for 30 minutes. Combine slaw ingredients and toss with dressing. Taste for seasoning and add more salt and pepper if you wish. *Yield: About 4 cups.*

Celery Root Slaw

This is a wonderful winter slaw with a rich and pungent flavor. We love it with fresh pork roasted with apples, or with soups and sandwiches. It keeps well in the refrigerator for several days.

Slaw

½ medium celery root, peeled and diced (1 cup)
⅓ head white cabbage, shredded (2 cups)

Dressing

¼ cup Basic Mayonnaise (see page 67) or
    purchased mayonnaise
¼ cup sour cream
2 tablespoons sweet gherkins, minced
2 tablespoons fresh parsley, minced
1 teaspoon fresh tarragon leaves, minced
2 teaspoons fresh lemon juice
½ teaspoon capers, drained
½ teaspoon prepared Dijon mustard

Boil diced celery root in salted water in covered pot for about 5 minutes, or until tender. Drain and cool the celery root and toss with shredded cabbage. Whisk dressing ingredients together until smooth, pour over slaw, and mix well. Add salt and pepper if you wish. *Yield: 3 cups.*

Old-Fashioned Carrot Raisin Slaw

We love this traditional favorite with cold baked ham or grilled cheese sandwiches. This one is a good choice for a cold buffet, or for a lunch box! It keeps well in the refrigerator for several days.

Slaw

6 carrots, shredded (about 2 cups)
½ cup raisins

Dressing

½ cup Basic Mayonnaise (see page 67) or
*   purchased mayonnaise*
1 tablespoon sweet onion, grated
1 tablespoon apple cider vinegar
½ tablespoon honey

Toss the carrots and raisins in a bowl. Whisk together the dressing ingredients, and then pour over the carrots and raisins, and toss the slaw thoroughly. Add salt and pepper if you wish. *Yield: About 2½ cups.*

Celery and Carrot Slaw

This is a simple light salad for a hot summer day. It goes especially well with fried chicken. This slaw keeps in the refrigerator for several days.

Slaw

6 carrots, shredded (2 cups)
½ head fresh celery stalks, thinly sliced (2 cups)
1 scallion, thinly sliced

Dressing

½ cup plain yogurt
2 tablespoons Basic Mayonnaise (see page 67)
    or purchased mayonnaise
½ teaspoon caraway seeds, toasted and crushed
1 tablespoon fresh thyme leaves, minced

Toss slaw vegetables together in a deep bowl. Whisk together dressing ingredients until smooth, pour over slaw, and toss to combine well. Add salt and pepper if you wish. *Yield: 4 cups.*

Red Pepper Slaw

This is a great accompaniment to grilled shrimp or roasted chicken. It keeps well in the refrigerator for several days.

Slaw

1 medium red bell pepper, roasted, peeled, seeded, and
    julienned (see pages 176–77)
1 medium red bell pepper, julienned (1 cup)
½ medium Savoy cabbage, shredded (3 to 4 cups)
1 small red onion, thinly sliced (1 cup)

Dressing

⅓ cup Basic Mayonnaise (see page 67) or
    purchased mayonnaise
2 teaspoons white wine vinegar
½ cup sweet gherkins, thinly sliced
2 garlic cloves, minced

Toss roasted and raw peppers, cabbage, and onions in a large bowl. Whisk dressing ingredients together and pour over the slaw. Mix well, taste for seasoning, and add salt and pepper if you wish. *Yield: 5 cups.*

Orange Onion Slaw

This spicy slaw is unusual and refreshing. Serve it with hot or cold roasted turkey, chicken, or pork. It should be served immediately after assembling.

Slaw

2 sweet oranges, sectioned, all pith and membrane removed (1½ cups)
1 small red onion, sliced into thin rings (1 cup)
¼ head Napa cabbage, cut into ¼-inch chiffonade (2 cups)
1 tablespoon fresh parsley, minced
¼ cup pomegranate seeds (optional)

Dressing

1 tablespoon fresh orange juice
2 tablespoons red wine vinegar
1 teaspoon honey
⅛ teaspoon ground cinnamon
1 generous pinch ground cloves
1 pinch salt
1 pinch freshly ground black pepper
⅓ cup canola oil

Put the orange sections in a sieve over a bowl to drain thoroughly. Roll up the sections in a clean dish towel and chill. Using a sharp knife, slice the cabbage crosswise into ¼-inch chiffonade (you should have about 2 cups) and chill. Whisk the dressing ingredients together, adding oil in a steady stream to make a thick emulsion, and then set aside.

Place the sliced onion in a small, deep bowl, pour the dressing over the onion and marinate at room temperature about 30 minutes. When ready to serve, combine ingredients in a salad bowl and toss gently. Add salt and pepper if you wish. *Yield: About 3 cups.*

Sesame Mushroom Slaw

A delicious Asian-style slaw, we serve this with grilled beef or tuna steaks. It's best served the same day you make it, chilled or at room temperature.

Slaw

¼ head Napa cabbage, shredded (about 2 cups)
2 scallions, thinly sliced on the diagonal
½ cup straw mushrooms, washed and dried
½ cup oyster mushrooms, julienned
½ cup water chestnuts, thinly sliced

Dressing

3 tablespoons sesame seeds, toasted
2 tablespoons soy sauce
2 tablespoons red wine vinegar
1 teaspoon honey
1 teaspoon sesame oil
⅓ cup peanut or canola oil

Combine vegetables in a large bowl. Place toasted sesame seeds in a mortar, grind thoroughly, and then transfer to a mixing bowl. In a small bowl, dissolve honey in soy sauce and vinegar. Slowly whisk soy and vinegar mixture into the ground sesame seeds, and then whisk the oils into the dressing. Pour dressing over slaw and toss. Add salt and pepper if you wish. *Yield: About 3 cups.*

Black-Eyed Pea Slaw

This is nice served on New Year's Day with a cold buffet of meats and cheeses. It keeps well for several days in the refrigerator.

Slaw

2 cups cooked black-eyed peas
½ small white cabbage, shredded (3 cups)
3 carrots, grated (1 cup)
¼ cup shallots, finely chopped
2 large garlic cloves, minced

Dressing

1 cup fresh parsley, minced
¼ cup white wine vinegar
3 tablespoons prepared Dijon mustard
¾ cup canola oil

Combine slaw vegetables in a large bowl. Whisk together dressing ingredients while adding oil in a steady stream to make an emulsion. Pour the dressing over the slaw and mix well. Add salt and pepper if you wish. *Yield: 5 cups.*

Carolina Barbecue Slaw

This sassy slaw is traditionally served with Carolina shredded pork barbecue on what is unabashedly called a "pig sandwich." But it's also great with any grilled or barbecued meats, or as a luncheon side dish with deli sandwiches. It keeps in the refrigerator for a week or more.

Slaw

¼ head white cabbage, shredded (2 cups)
3 carrots, shredded (1 cup)

Dressing

½ cup vinegar
2 tablespoons honey
¼ teaspoon freshly ground black pepper
⅛ teaspoon salt
⅛ teaspoon hot red chile powder

Simmer the vinegar, honey, pepper, salt and chile powder over a medium flame until honey is dissolved. Cool the dressing, then pour over the shredded vegetables and toss to combine thoroughly. Add salt and pepper if you wish. *Yield: About 3 cups.*

Marinated Cucumber Slaw

This zesty caraway-flavored slaw is a favorite with cold poached
sea bass or salmon, and it goes well with grilled meats as well. The
cucumbers can be marinated for several days in the refrigerator,
but once the slaw is mixed it should be served right away.

Slaw

1 large cucumber, peeled, seeded, and julienned (1 cup)
¼ head small white cabbage, shredded (1½ cups)
½ cup water chestnuts, diced
2 to 3 tablespoons canola oil

Marinade

¼ cup white wine
¼ cup white wine vinegar
½ tablespoon honey
1 teaspoon caraway seeds, toasted and crushed
¼ teaspoon salt
⅛ teaspoon freshly ground black pepper

Combine vinegar, wine, honey, caraway seeds, and salt and
pepper in a small bowl and whisk until honey dissolves. Pour
marinade over the cucumbers and cover. Chill 4 to 6 hours; stir
occasionally.

When ready to serve, toss cabbage and water chestnuts with
oil in a large bowl. Drain the cucumbers (reserving marinade)
and toss with the cabbage. Drizzle marinade over the slaw by
tablespoons, tossing, until it is nicely dressed but not dripping.
Add salt and pepper if you wish. Serve immediately. *Yield:
About 3 cups.*

Mango Chile Slaw

This sparkling, golden fruit slaw goes beautifully with grilled fresh fish. It's best made just before serving.

3 firm mangoes, peeled and julienned (3 cups)
1 poblano chile, roasted, peeled, seeded, and
    julienned (see pages 176–77)
1 small red onion, diced (1 cup)
6 scallions, thinly sliced on the diagonal
¼ cup fresh lime juice
3 tablespoons fresh cilantro leaves, chopped
1 teaspoon chile Caribe flakes

Combine ingredients gently and chill for an hour. Add salt and pepper if you wish. *Yield: About 4 cups.*

CRUNCHY, SAVORY GREENS!

For much of the year, groceries and farmers' market stands present such a delectable variety of cabbages, lettuces, greens, and herbs that salads and slaws never have to be ho-hum again. Savory cabbage slaws—easy, inexpensive accompaniments to most meals—can be based on good old-fashioned white or red cabbages (lots of crunch and strong cabbage flavor) or on their more exotic cousins. Savoy cabbage is more subtle in flavor, with a beautiful round head of dark green leaves marked by a lacy pattern of veins. Napa and Chinese cabbages, pale green to nearly white, form an elongated head of crinkled leaves that we stack up and cut crosswise into a delicate chiffonade. Beyond the humble cabbage, the "chopped salad" concept has moved uptown and taken on a whole new wardrobe of savory greens. We have included slaws based on Romaine lettuce, fresh spinach, and peppery arugula. In addition, try adding some sharply flavored escarole, chard, endive, kale, broccoli rabe, frisee, or mustard, turnip, or dandelion greens to your slaw as substitutes for some of the cabbage or lettuce called for. If you have a good farmers' market nearby, your creative options will be endless!

Apple, Carrot, and Pecan Slaw

Serve this colorful, warm slaw with pot roast, or pork loin or chops. It will keep a day or two in the refrigerator. Rewarm the slaw gently before serving.

> 4 tablespoons pecans, toasted and chopped
> 3 tablespoons butter
> 3 large green apples, julienned (3 cups)
> 2 large carrots, julienned (1 cup)
> 1 small red onion, thinly sliced lengthwise (1 cup)
> 4 tablespoons water
> 3 teaspoons raw sugar
> ¼ teaspoon salt

In a large skillet sauté pecans in butter over moderately high flame, stirring until golden. Transfer with a slotted spoon to a paper towel to drain. Add apple, carrot, and onion to the skillet and sauté while stirring for 1 minute. Add remaining ingredients and simmer uncovered until carrot is just tender, or 3 to 4 minutes. Add pepper and more salt if you wish. Stir in pecans and serve. *Yield: 3 cups.*

Jicama, Carrot, and Peanut Slaw

This slaw has great texture and unusual flavor combinations. We especially like it as a side salad with grilled fish. It should be served as soon as you put it together.

Slaw

1 medium jicama, peeled and julienned (2 cups)
3 large carrots, peeled and shredded (1 cup)
½ medium red onion, finely chopped (⅔ cup)
¼ cup parsley, minced
¼ cup peanuts, toasted

Dressing

¼ cup fresh lime juice
1 tablespoon raw sugar
½ teaspoon freshly-cracked black pepper
⅛ teaspoon hot red chile powder
½ cup peanut or canola oil

Toss vegetables together in a large bowl. Whisk dressing ingredients together, adding oil in a thin stream to make an emulsion. Pour dressing over the slaw and mix well. Add salt and pepper if you wish. *Yield: 4 cups.*

Spinach Slaw with Peaches

This slaw makes a great luncheon dish and is endlessly variable—make it with pears, plums, strawberries, raspberries, or melon instead of (or in addition to) peaches. The bite of the spinach is the perfect counterpoint to the sweet soft flesh of summer fruits. Serve it immediately after assembling.

Slaw

1 bunch fresh spinach, washed, stemmed, and
    dried (2 cups packed)
3 peaches, firm but ripe (2 cups, sliced)
½ cup water chestnuts, roughly chopped
1 large scallion

Dressing

1 tablespoon balsamic vinegar
2 tablespoons rice vinegar
1 tablespoon honey
½ teaspoon soy sauce
1 tablespoon sesame seeds, lightly toasted
1 teaspoon sesame oil
3 tablespoons peanut oil

Whisk the dressing ingredients together and add oil in a steady stream to make a thick emulsion. Set the dressing aside in a deep bowl.

Drop the peaches in boiling water for 10 seconds and slip off their skins. Slice the peaches into sections and add them to the dressing, stirring to coat the peaches. Stack the spinach leaves and slice lengthwise into ¼ inch chiffonade. Slice the scallion crosswise into 2-inch pieces, and then slice each piece lengthwise into shreds.

When ready to serve, combine all ingredients in a large bowl and toss gently. Add salt and pepper if you wish. *Yield: 4 to 5 cups.*

Gingered Asparagus Slaw

This delicious and colorful warm slaw is great for a buffet table or an elegant supper party. It should be served soon after you've put it together.

1 pound asparagus spears, trimmed (16 to 20 spears)
⅓ cup peanut or canola oil
1 large garlic clove, peeled and crushed
1 1-inch piece fresh ginger, peeled and finely chopped
1 red bell pepper, julienned (1 cup)
4 scallions, thinly sliced on diagonal
½ medium jicama, peeled and julienned (1 cup)
2 tablespoons rice vinegar
2 tablespoons soy sauce
1 teaspoon hot chile oil

Steam the trimmed asparagus spears for 3 to 5 minutes or until barely crisp-tender. Plunge the spears into ice water to cool, and then drain thoroughly. Cut the asparagus into 2-inch lengths, then cut lengthwise into julienne strips. You should have about 2 cups.

In a wok or deep skillet, heat the oil until hot but not smoking. Toss in the garlic and ginger and cook, stirring, for 1 minute. Toss in the asparagus and cook, stirring, for 2 minutes. Toss in remaining vegetables, stir, and cut off the flame. Sprinkle the vinegar, soy sauce, and hot oil over the vegetables and toss thoroughly. Add salt and pepper if you wish. *Yield: About 3½ cups.*

Celery Root, Apple, and Gruyère Slaw

We love this crunchy, cool slaw with a slow-cooked, barbecued beef brisket. And it makes a zesty lunch with a cup of good soup and a baguette. It will keep in the refrigerator up to 24 hours before serving.

Slaw

½ medium celery root, peeled and julienned (1 cup)
1 large green apple, peeled and julienned (1 cup)
¼ pound Gruyère cheese, julienned
1 tablespoon fresh lemon juice
¼ head white cabbage, shredded (2 cups)

Dressing

¼ cup Basic Mayonnaise (see page 67) or
    purchased mayonnaise
2 tablespoons sour cream
1 tablespoon prepared Dijon mustard
1 tablespoon fresh horseradish, grated
1 tablespoon honey
½ teaspoon salt

Toss the celery root, apple, cheese, and lemon juice together in a large bowl. Add the cabbage, toss again, and set aside. Whisk dressing ingredients together until well combined and pour over the slaw. Toss, taste for seasoning, and add pepper and more salt if you wish. *Yield: About 4 cups.*

Wilted Red Cabbage Slaw

This is a sweet tangy slaw with wonderful flavor that we often serve with grilled sausages. It's best served right after you make it.

½ pound lean bacon, cut into 1-inch pieces
¼ cup balsamic vinegar
½ cup water
1 tablespoon prepared Dijon mustard
1 tablespoon honey
1 tablespoon caraway seeds
¼ teaspoon freshly ground black pepper
1 small head red cabbage, shredded fine (5 to 6 cups)

Sauté the bacon until crisp, drain, and set aside. In a large kettle, bring vinegar and water to a boil. Whisk in mustard, honey, caraway seeds, and pepper. Reduce flame and stir cabbage into the pot, simmering for 3 to 5 minutes, or until cabbage is wilted but still has a little crunch. Add the reserved bacon and toss to combine. Add salt and more pepper if you wish. Serve hot or cool to room temperature. *Yield: 5 to 6 cups.*

Roasted Winter Vegetable Slaw

This rich, aromatic slaw is a beautiful and filling side dish for winter meals, and it goes especially well with pork roast or a whole roasted chicken. It's substantial enough to serve as a vegetarian meal in itself. It should be served at room temperature or slightly warm, right after you put it together.

> ¼ small cauliflower, julienned (about 1 cup)
> 1 large carrot, julienned
> 1 large golden beet, julienned
> 1 parsnip, julienned
> 2 garlic cloves, minced
> 1½ tablespoons fresh parsley, minced
> 1½ tablespoons fresh rosemary leaves, minced
> ¼ teaspoon salt
> large pinch ground pepper
> ⅓ cup olive oil
> 2 tablespoons balsamic vinegar
> ½ cup red cabbage, shredded

Preheat oven to 325 degrees F. Toss all ingredients (except red cabbage) together in a bowl to thoroughly combine. Spread vegetables in a shallow roasting pan and roast for about an hour, or until just crisp-tender. Let vegetables cool to room temperature, and then toss with red cabbage. Add more salt and pepper if you wish. *Yield: About 2½ cups.*

Spicy Snow Pea Slaw and Egg Ribbons

This unusual Asian-style slaw is good with both seafood and grilled meats. It should be served as soon as it's put together.

Slaw

2 eggs, beaten with 2 tablespoons ice water
2 tablespoons vegetable oil
½ pound snow peas, trimmed (1 cup)
3 tender inner stalks of celery, julienned
1 red bell pepper, julienned (about 1 cup)
2 tablespoons fresh parsley, minced

Dressing

2 tablespoons red wine vinegar
2 tablespoons soy sauce
1 teaspoon red chile powder
1 garlic clove, minced
4 tablespoons peanut or canola oil

Heat the vegetable oil in a 10-inch non-stick skillet until medium hot. Pour the eggs into the skillet and tilt the pan so that the eggs cover the bottom. Reduce the flame and cook the eggs very slowly without disturbing them until they are cooked through and nearly dry on top—but do not let the bottom scorch! Remove from the flame and set aside until the eggs have cooled Gently slide the eggs onto a flat surface, roll into a cylinder, cover with a damp cloth, and chill.

Steam the snow peas until tender-crisp, about 2 or 3 minutes, and plunge into ice water to cool. Drain and dry thoroughly. Combine snow peas with celery, bell pepper, and parsley and toss.

Whisk the dressing ingredients together and pour over the vegetables. Cover and chill for an hour or two. Bring the slaw to room temperature and toss. Add salt and pepper if you wish. Just before serving, slice the rolled eggs crosswise into ¼-inch strips, unroll them, and very gently mix them into the slaw. *Yield: About 3 cups.*

Warm Cabbage and Mushroom Slaw

This is a good winter slaw to go with beef or pork tenderloin, or on its own. Serve it warm or at room temperature, as soon as you've put it together.

½ cup white wine vinegar
½ cup water
¼ cup raw sugar
¾ teaspoon salt
½ teaspoon prepared Dijon mustard
1 pound white mushrooms, sliced (2 cups)
1 red bell pepper, sliced into 1-inch strips (1 cup)
1 shallot, chopped
3 tablespoons olive oil
1 tablespoon mustard seeds
¼ head red cabbage, shredded (1½ cups)

Bring vinegar, water, and sugar to a boil in a small saucepan. Add salt and mustard, and simmer for about 3 minutes while stirring occasionally. In a large, heavy skillet sauté mushrooms, red peppers, and shallots in oil over medium-high flame for about 10 minutes or until browned. Add mustard seeds and sauté about 2 minutes or until the seeds begin to pop. Add vinegar mixture and simmer 1 minute. Stir in cabbage and simmer another 2 minutes, or until just wilted. Drain vegetables over a saucepan and set vegetables aside. Boil the liquid over medium-high flame until reduced to about 3 tablespoons, and then stir into the vegetables. Add salt and pepper if you wish. *Yield: About 3 cups.*

Beet, Arugula, and Goat Cheese Slaw

This unusual and flavorful slaw makes a great side salad for a steak or chop, or a good luncheon dish on its own. Be sure to use the freshest baby arugula—mature arugula will make the slaw intolerably bitter. The slaw should be served within a few hours of assembling.

Slaw

¼ cup walnuts
1 teaspoon ground cumin
¼ teaspoon salt
¼ teaspoon white pepper
4 medium beets, cooked, peeled, and julienned
2 cups fresh baby arugula, washed and dried
4 ounces goat cheese, crumbled

Dressing

1½ tablespoons prepared Dijon mustard
½ teaspoon fresh tarragon leaves, minced
2 tablespoons white wine vinegar
¼ cup plus 2 tablespoons extra virgin olive oil

Toss walnuts with cumin, salt, and pepper, and then lightly toast the nuts (see page 180). In large bowl toss together walnuts, beets, arugula, and crumbled goat cheese. Whisk dressing ingredients together, adding olive oil in a thin stream to make an emulsion. Pour dressing over the slaw and mix well. Add salt and pepper if you wish. *Yield: About 5 cups.*

Portobello Mushroom and White Bean Slaw

This simple vegetarian slaw is an elegant appetizer served warm with savory crackers. We also love it as a hearty luncheon or supper main dish with slices of crusty bread drizzled with olive oil, sprinkled with grated Parmesan cheese and toasted. Serve it immediately once you've put it together.

2 tablespoons butter
1 large portobello mushroom cap, cleaned and
*   thinly sliced*
2 shallots, minced
½ cup balsamic vinegar
1 teaspoon prepared Dijon mustard
2 tablespoons honey
¼ head Savoy cabbage, thinly sliced (2 cups)
2 cups cooked white beans, drained and warm
3 Roma tomatoes, seeded and diced (1 cup)

Melt butter in a large skillet and sauté the mushrooms and shallots over medium flame for 3 minutes (the mushrooms should still be firm). Stir in vinegar, mustard, and honey, and cook 3 minutes. Add the cabbage and toss gently, cooking for about 2 more minutes. Turn off the flame, add the warm beans and diced tomato, and toss. Add salt and pepper if you wish.
Yield: About 4 cups.

Prosciutto and Melon Slaw

This wonderful fresh slaw is best served with a simple omelet or on its own with crusty bread and a chilled white wine. Your guests will be back for more! The slaw should be served as soon as it is combined.

½ small honeydew melon, julienned
¼ cup dried figs
¼ cup currants
3 tablespoons Grand Marnier or orange liqueur
4 ounces prosciutto, cut in a thick slab, then julienned
4 tablespoons fresh mint leaves, minced

Place the julienned honeydew in a sieve to drain thoroughly. Slice figs in half and soak figs and currants in Grand Marnier for 15 minutes, or until liqueur is almost fully absorbed. Gently toss ingredients together, taste for seasoning, and add salt and pepper if you wish. *Yield: 2¾ cups.*

Chicken Caesar Slaw

This popular dish makes a wonderful light lunch or supper. It's best made with freshly broiled chicken breasts cut into julienne strips while still warm from the broiler. The dressing can be made ahead and kept chilled for several days. Bring it back to room temperature before serving.

Slaw

1 head Romaine lettuce, cut crosswise in ¼-inch
    chiffonade (6 or 7 cups)
4 chicken breast halves, broiled and julienned
1 small red onion, sliced into thin rings (1 cup)
½ cup croutons

Dressing

½ cup olive oil
1 garlic clove, pressed
1 egg
1 lemon, juiced
6 anchovy fillets, minced
½ cup Parmesan cheese, grated
⅛ teaspoon salt

Press or crush the garlic into the oil and let stand 30 minutes. Drop the egg into boiling water just until coddled (20 to 30 seconds), and then break the egg into a food processor or deep bowl. Process or whisk the egg for about 10 seconds, and then add the garlic olive oil by drops until the mixture begins to thicken. Increase oil to a thin stream until it is incorporated. Toss in the lemon juice, anchovy, cheese, and salt to blend.

To assemble the slaw, toss Romaine chiffonade with chicken, onion and croutons in a large bowl. Drizzle enough dressing over the bowl to coat the chiffonade lightly, and mix well. Add pepper and more salt if you wish. *Yield: 6 to 7 cups.*

Chicken and Raspberry Slaw

Fresh spinach chiffonade is a lovely base for a light fruit slaw. For this recipe, we've turned it into a meal by adding tender breast of chicken, fresh from the grill. The dressing can be made a day or two ahead and kept chilled, and then brought to room temperature before proceeding. The slaw should be served immediately after assembling.

Slaw

1 bunch fresh spinach, washed, stemmed, and dried
4 chicken breast halves, grilled and thinly sliced
2 cups fresh raspberries, washed and dried
½ cup whole almonds, toasted and slivered
1 small red onion, sliced into thin rings (1 cup)

Dressing

2 tablespoons raspberry vinegar
2 tablespoons red wine vinegar
1 teaspoon prepared Dijon mustard
1 teaspoon honey
1 pinch salt
1 pinch freshly ground black pepper
½ cup canola oil

Whisk dressing ingredients together, adding oil in a thin stream to make an emulsion. Set dressing aside for 30 minutes. Stack spinach leaves and slice lengthwise into ¼-inch chiffonade; chill. Grill the chicken breasts, let stand to cool about 3 minutes, and then slice diagonally into thin strips. Combine slaw ingredients in a large salad bowl, pour dressing over slaw, and toss gently. Taste for seasoning and add more salt and pepper if you wish.
Yield: 7 to 8 cups.

Beef and Blue Cheese Slaw

For this elegant combination, use really good and freshly roasted beef cooked rare. It makes a grand meal in itself, with crusty bread and a good red wine. Serve the slaw soon after you've made it.

Slaw
½ head Napa cabbage, cut in ¼ inch chiffonade
    (about 4 cups)
1 bunch fresh chives, cut into 1 inch lengths (½ cup)
½ red bell pepper, finely julienned (½ cup)
2 cups rare roast of beef, julienned and marinated
    (see below)
½ cup blue cheese, crumbled

Dressing
4 tablespoons red wine vinegar
2 tablespoons fresh parsley, minced
1 teaspoon red chile powder
⅛ teaspoon salt
1 pinch freshly ground pepper
½ cup olive oil

Whisk the dressing ingredients together, adding oil in a slow stream to make an emulsion. Pour the dressing over the julienned beef in a deep bowl, toss well, and set aside to marinate at room temperature for 30 minutes. To serve, toss the beef with remaining ingredients in a large bowl. Add pepper and more salt if you wish. *Yield: 6 to 7 cups.*

Lamb and Walnut Slaw

This rich, warm slaw makes a lovely winter supper for special guests. Serve it with crusty country bread and a good red wine. The dressing can be made ahead and kept chilled for several days. Bring it to warm room temperature before proceeding to assemble the slaw. The slaw should be served warm as soon as it's put together.

Slaw
1 garlic clove, pressed
6 tablespoons olive oil
½ head Romaine lettuce, washed and dried
1 cup watercress leaves, washed and dried
1 large portobello mushroom, washed, dried,
    and julienned
½ cup Herbed Walnuts (see page 182)
1 teaspoon fresh rosemary leaves, minced
2 cups freshly roasted leg of lamb, julienned,
    at room temperature

Dressing
1½ tablespoons prepared Dijon mustard
3 tablespoons balsamic vinegar
1½ teaspoons fresh rosemary leaves, minced
¼ teaspoon salt
1 pinch freshly ground black pepper
4 tablespoons walnut oil

Press or crush the garlic into the olive oil and let stand 30 minutes. With a sharp knife, slice the Romaine crosswise into ¼ inch chiffonade, toss with the watercress, and chill. In a large salad bowl, whisk dressing ingredients together, adding oil in a thin stream to make an emulsion. Cover the dressing and set aside.

In a heavy skillet, brown the julienne strips of mushroom in 2 tablespoons of the garlic oil over a medium flame for about 3 minutes, or until slightly browned. Stir in the walnuts and rosemary, sprinkle with a little salt and pepper, and cook while stirring, for another 3 or 4 minutes. Pour the mushrooms and walnuts into the dressing, cover, and set aside. Place the julienned lamb into the skillet with 1 tablespoon of the garlic oil and warm for 2 to 3 minutes while stirring and tossing. Add the lamb to the dressing and toss.

Stir the greens into the mushroom and lamb mixture and toss gently, adding more garlic oil by spoonfuls if necessary to coat the chiffonade well. Taste for seasoning and add more salt and pepper if you wish. *Yield: 7 or 8 cups.*

What's for Dinner?

Perfect Pasta

What could be simpler, faster, and more delicious than pasta for supper? And we've come such a long way from good old spaghetti and meatballs! Pasta, made from a "paste" of wheat flour and egg or water, makes a substantial and healthy meal you can put on the table in practically no time at all—dressed up with a rich sauce or pesto, dressed down in a simple coat of olive oil and chopped parsley, or chilled in ice water and tossed with fresh vegetables in a savory vinaigrette. The trick, of course, is to have a selection of good dried pastas on hand in the pantry.

We believe in basic dried pasta made from good semolina flour and water. All pastas are not the same quality or flavor, so you should shop around until you find the brand that works best for you. Our preference is for De Cecco, an Italian brand that's been around for over 100 years and is widely available in markets all over the country. Long round strands of extruded pasta, such as spaghetti, spaghettini, and vermicelli, are among the most popular and widely available dried pastas. Among "noodles"—flat ribbons of pasta of varying widths and lengths—fettuccini, linguine, tagliatelli, and lasagna seem to be available everywhere. Popular "tubes" of pasta include macaroni, ziti, penne, rigatoni, cannelloni, and great big manicotti for stuffing. Among popular shapes for pasta salads are corkscrew-shaped fusilli, twisted strands of gemelli, rotelle (or wheels), conchiglie (shells), orecchiette (ears?), orzo, and farfalle (which look like butterflies or bowties). There are literally dozens of different dried pasta shapes and sizes, but they are all made of the same "paste," all last virtually forever on the pantry shelf, and all are cooked the same way.

Today, you can find colorful pastas made with tomatoes, spinach, and chile peppers, and even black pastas made with squid ink. From our point of view, most of these fad pastas look interesting on the table but offer no bonus in flavor over ordinary dried pasta. We also see no particular advantage to buying refrigerated fresh pastas, except that they cook a little faster. We have found that some of them are quite good, but not better than dried pastas.

How to Cook Pasta

Bring at least 5 quarts of fresh cold water to a rolling boil in a large pot, preferably stainless steel. Toss in 2 tablespoons of salt, or more if you wish. Do not put any oil in the water. Put the pasta in the water and partially cover to quickly bring the water back to a rolling boil. Cook until the pasta is done "al dente" or to the consistency you prefer, or 5 to 15 minutes for dried pasta, depending on the size and shape of the pasta. To our taste, the pasta is "done" when the water begins to foam.

When the pasta is done, drain it immediately. Do not let it stand in hot water. If your pot has a pasta sieve, simply lift it out to drain the pasta. Otherwise, pour the contents of the pot into a colander to drain. Serve the pasta immediately. There are fancy pasta "forks" available for tossing and serving, but they're hard to clean and they have no other use, so ours got lost in the gadget drawer long ago. We use our handy, multi-purpose metal tongs and pay the price of breaking a strand or two on occasion.

If you must hold the pasta for a few minutes before serving, toss it with a few tablespoons of olive oil, put it in a warmed bowl, cover with foil, and keep in a warm oven (about 200 degrees F) until ready to serve.

If you are using the pasta for a cold salad, drain it and then pour the drained pasta into a bowl of ice water. Stir it up with your hands for a minute or two, then drain thoroughly in a colander, mix and dress the salad, and serve. If you must keep the cooked pasta for a while before mixing your salad together, pour it into a deep bowl lined with a dishcloth, cover it with plastic wrap, and store in the refrigerator for up to an hour or two. Always serve pasta very freshly cooked. If it sits in the refrigerator for several hours the flavor and texture will deteriorate, and it may turn sour.

Filled pastas are another matter altogether, of course. We have been known to make our own ravioli or cappelletti for very grand occasions, or to stash in the freezer for emergencies. But when time is a factor we buy a good brand of fresh filled pasta at the grocery or a good Italian delicatessen. Fresh filled pastas can be cooked in about 5 minutes, and that's hard to beat! You can make your own filled pastas and flat noodles very simply and without any special equipment. Although it's messy and may take a couple of hours the first time around, it's fun to do and very rewarding to be able to serve your own handmade pasta.

How to Make Your Own Noodles and Filled Pasta

Pile 1½ cups of all-purpose flour on a smooth work surface, such as a kitchen counter, and keep additional flour handy. Sprinkle ¼ teaspoon salt over the flour, and make a well in the middle of the flour with steep even sides. Crack 2 eggs into the well and gently stir up the eggs with a fork until they are well mixed. While still using the fork, gradually mix the flour into the eggs from the sides of the well until you have incorporated all the flour into a slightly sticky dough. Abandon the fork, flour your hands, and knead the dough for 10 minutes, adding more flour as necessary to keep it from sticking to your hands, the counter, the kitchen drawers, and so forth. Divide the dough in half and set aside.

Clean up the work surface, scraping up any bits of dough so that it's clean and dry. Dust the surface with flour. Using a floured rolling pin, roll out one piece of dough into a very, very, very thin sheet (paper-thin if you can get there) about 9 inches wide and 15 inches long. Pick it up on the rolling pin and unroll it on a floured dish cloth to dry for 15 to 20 minutes. Repeat the procedure with the second piece of dough.

Noodles

To make noodles, roll one sheet of dough into a long cylinder. With a sharp knife, slice the cylinder crosswise into strips the width you want (e.g., less than ¼ inch wide for fettuccini, and 2 to 3 inches wide for lasagna). Repeat the process with the remaining dough. Unroll the strands and let them air dry until you can handle them easily; one way is to hang the ribbons over a broom handle suspended across the backs of a couple of kitchen chairs. Collect the ribbons, wrap them gently in plastic wrap, pop into a freezer bag and refrigerate or freeze until ready to cook. Fresh pasta will keep in the refrigerator for three or four days, and in the freezer for several months.

Ravioli

To make ravioli, cut each sheet of dough lengthwise into 3 3-inch strips. Place scant tablespoons of filling along the center of one strip 1½ to 2 inches apart. Using a pastry brush or your finger dipped in a little water, moisten the long edges of the strip and the spaces between the spoons of filling. Carefully lay another strip of dough over the filled strip and press down the edges and between mounds of filling to seal. With a sharp knife, cut between the mounds and press the cut edges again to seal. Lay out the ravioli on a floured cloth to air dry for 30 minutes, turning them occasionally so they dry on both sides. Cook them, or wrap them gently in plastic wrap, pop into a freezer bag, and refrigerate or freeze until ready to cook. We don't keep fresh filled pasta in the icebox for more than a day or two, but generally it will keep in the freezer for several months, depending on the type of filling.

Cappelletti

To make cappelletti, cut circles of dough, 2½ to 3 inches in diameter, with a cookie cutter. Place ½ tablespoon of filling just off-center on each circle. Brush the edges of the dough with water, using a pastry brush or your finger, and carefully fold the dough in half over the filling to make a semi-circle, pressing down the edges to seal. When all the dough has been filled, make the "caps" by picking up a semi-circle and folding it gently around your finger so the two corners of the semi-circle overlap. Dab the overlapping corners with water and press together to seal. Lay out the cappelletti on a floured cloth to air dry for 30 minutes, turning them occasionally so they dry on both sides. Cook them, or wrap them gently in plastic wrap, pop into a freezer bag, and refrigerate or freeze until ready to cook. Cook them within a day or two, or keep them in the freezer for several months, depending on the type of filling.

Quick Chicken

The typical busy cook has learned to rely on quick and easy chicken dishes. Chicken is readily available, inexpensive, low in fat and cholesterol, freezes well, defrosts quickly, and everybody seems to like it. Sautéed, fried, poached, braised, roasted, or grilled—chicken is the perfect foil for a pungent or fiery sauce, salsa, or slaw.

As a precaution, remember to handle raw chicken as little as possible, as quickly as possible, and with care. Keep it well chilled until immediately before cooking. Store it in the refrigerator tightly wrapped and separated from other foods. Always wash your hands, knives, cutting board, and other utensils and equipment in hot sudsy water after handling raw chicken.

For everyday cooking we buy fresh whole fryers (never previously frozen), take them home in a bag of ice, and freeze them right away. With a good sharp chef's knife and a little experience, it's easy to dismember a 2- or 3-pound chicken, and we often do several at a time (keeping everything well iced except the pieces we're working on). We trim, rinse, and dry the pieces carefully; wrap each tightly in butcher's paper or plastic wrap; place them on the floor of the freezer, widely separated, until frozen; and then seal them into a heavy-duty freezer bag until they're needed. We load the backs, wings, and bones (if we've boned out the breast meat, for example) into the stock pot right away, or freeze them to make soup later. We may coat some of the pieces with a good dry rub or thick marinade and let them stand 30 minutes, covered, in the refrigerator before freezing. We try to label the freezer bag with the rub or marinade we've used so there aren't any surprises!

For only a little more money, "economy packs" of bone-in or boneless breasts, thighs, and drumsticks are readily available either fresh or already frozen. If we buy fresh chicken (not previously frozen), we rewrap and freeze the pieces in meal-size packages. If we buy frozen, we keep the chicken frozen in its original packaging. In either case, we use it within two or three months. If you own a powerful, sub-zero deep freezer you can keep frozen poultry for much longer.

Freezing chicken has the disadvantage of releasing some of the juices of the meat and allowing them to escape in the defrosting process. It's best to defrost chicken slowly if possible. If you transfer a 1-pound package of chicken from the freezer to the refrigerator at night, it should be nearly defrosted by the next evening. If you have to defrost chicken quickly, seal it into a fresh freezer bag and submerge the bag in a sink of lukewarm water for about 10 minutes, then separate the pieces and let stand until fully defrosted. Audrey pops chicken into her microwave oven and gives it no more than 3 minutes on the turntable at a "defrost" setting, then lets it stand until it is defrosted. (You'll have to figure out the time and setting that works best for your own microwave.) If you have marinated the chicken before freezing, wipe the rub or marinade off the meat before proceeding to cook. Chicken should be brought to cool room temperature before cooking.

Sautéed Chicken

Bring the chicken to cool room temperature and pat dry with paper towels. Sprinkle with salt and pepper if you wish.

Heat ½ tablespoon of olive oil and ½ tablespoon of butter in a heavy skillet over medium-high flame until the butter foams and is hot but not smoking. Put the chicken pieces in the pan and sear quickly, about 3 minutes on each side, just until lightly browned. Reduce the flame to medium-low and sauté until the chicken pieces are cooked through but still tender and juicy. Boneless breasts may be ready in 15 minutes; bone-in pieces will take about 30 minutes. If you have any doubts about whether it's done, cut into the meat near the bone. If it is still pink and shiny, it needs more cooking. Serve the chicken with a pungent salsa or slaw, or pour a grand sauce around the chicken and heat through.

Fried Chicken

In a deep bowl, whisk 1 egg with ½ cup of milk. In another bowl whisk 1 cup of all-purpose flour with ¼ teaspoon of salt, a few grindings of black pepper, and a good pinch or two of cayenne pepper. Pour canola or another neutral vegetable oil into a large, heavy, cast-iron skillet (preferably non-stick) that has a tight-fitting lid. Put the skillet over a medium-high flame to heat.

Meanwhile, pat the chicken pieces dry and dredge them in the seasoned flour, shaking to remove excess flour. Dip each floured chicken piece in the milk and egg bath, coating well, dredge in flour again, and set aside on a rack to dry a little.

The oil is hot enough when a bread cube tossed into the oil will sizzle madly (360 degrees F on a frying thermometer). Using tongs, carefully lay the chicken pieces into the skillet, skin side down. Cook until golden brown on all sides, turning several times, for a total of about 10 to 12 minutes. Turn the chicken pieces skin side up, reduce the flame to medium-low, carefully pour 3 or 4 tablespoons of water into the bottom of the skillet (watch out for spatters!) and cover the pan tightly. Cook the chicken for 25 minutes. Remove the cover, and continue cooking for another 5 to 10 minutes. Drain on paper towels. Fried chicken definitely calls for a zesty slaw.

Stove-Top Grilled Chicken

Boneless breasts are fine candidates for the stove-top grill. We like to soak them in a punchy marinade for 30 minutes before grilling.

Preheat a cast-iron or other heavy, ridged grill pan over medium-high flame until hot. Brush the ridges of the pan with a little olive oil and place the chicken breasts over the ridges. Cook about 3 minutes on each side or until done to your liking. Serve the breasts immediately with a great sauce, or let them stand 5 minutes and then slice them for a salad or into a sandwich.

Roasted Chicken

Roasting is perhaps the simplest treatment of all. You can roast a chicken of any size from 2 pounds or less to over 5 pounds, stuffed or unstuffed. Dry roasting, uncovered, at a very high temperature is the key to a crispy, golden brown skin and plump, juicy meat.

Preheat the oven to 475 degrees F. If the bird has been frozen, make sure that it is completely defrosted and brought to cool room temperature. Dry the bird thoroughly, inside and out. Stuff the bird, place a quartered onion and some fresh herbs such as rosemary or tarragon inside, or simply salt and pepper the cavity and leave it empty. Holding the bird breast side up, break the joint of the wing tip and gently twist the wings under the bird until they lock behind the back. Rub the outside with butter or a good olive oil and some minced fresh herbs.

Place the bird on a rack, breast side up, and place in a roasting pan just large enough to hold it comfortably. Roast the bird uncovered at 475 degrees F for 30 minutes, and then reduce heat to 350 degrees F and roast until done. A chicken under 2 pounds may be finished in another 15 or 20 minutes; a larger chicken will take longer. The bird is done when the internal temperature reaches 180 degrees F, and the juices run clear or yellow when the thickest part of the thigh is pierced to the bone. Let the bird stand 10 minutes before carving.

Braised Chicken

We don't recommend baking chicken pieces because it's too easy to end up with dried, tough meat. Braising, however, sears the skin and provides plenty of moisture to keep the meat juicy. Chicken pieces should be fully defrosted, brought to cool room temperature, and dried thoroughly with paper towels before beginning. Sprinkle the chicken with salt and pepper if you wish.

Preheat the oven to 325 degrees F. Heat ½ tablespoon of olive oil and ½ tablespoon of butter in a heavy skillet over medium-high flame until the butter foams and is hot but not smoking. Put the chicken pieces in the pan and sear quickly, about 3 minutes on each side, just until lightly browned. Transfer the chicken to paper towels to drain.

Pour the oil out of the skillet, reduce the flame to medium-low, and melt ½ stick of butter in the skillet. Finely dice 1 carrot, 1 stalk of celery, and half of a white onion, and toss together with 2 tablespoons of fresh parsley leaves, chopped. Sauté the vegetables in butter over a medium flame until wilted, about 7 minutes. If you have a thick vegetable or chile sauce available you can use the sauce instead of (or in addition to) the vegetables as a bed for braising the chicken.

Spread half the vegetables or sauce into a glass or ceramic casserole with a lid, just large enough to hold the chicken comfortably in a single layer. Arrange the browned chicken on the vegetables or sauce, and spread the remaining vegetables or sauce on top. Cover the casserole tightly and put in the oven. Pull out the casserole and test a piece for doneness after 30 minutes—timing will depend in part on the kind of casserole you're using. If the dish seems dry, add a little white wine or water to the bottom of the casserole. Return the dish to the oven, checking it every 5 minutes or so until done. If you have any doubts about whether the meat is cooked through, cut into the meat near the bone. If the meat is still pink and shiny, it needs more cooking. Serve the chicken in its braising sauce, or with a pungent salsa or slaw.

Poached Chicken

It's easy to poach chicken breasts for sandwiches, salads, mousses, and fillings. Place the breasts in a large enameled saucepan and cover with white wine, chicken stock, and water in equal parts. The liquid should cover the breasts by about an inch. If you wish, toss in a handful of fresh aromatic herbs, such as basil or tarragon. Do not add salt. Set the saucepan over a medium-high flame and bring to a boil. Reduce the flame to medium-low, partially cover the saucepan and simmer gently until the breasts are cooked through, or 10 to 12 minutes, depending on how many breasts you're poaching at once. The meat should be just barely past the pink stage and still tender. Remove the breasts to a plate to cool and discard the poaching liquid. The breasts can be used immediately, or wrapped and chilled for later use.

A whole poached chicken, cut up, can be covered in sauce and reheated in a hot oven to make a beautiful meal in less than an hour. To poach a whole stewing hen or fryer (3 to 5 pounds), cut up the bird and place it in a large stock pot. Add an onion, a carrot, and a celery stalk, all roughly chopped, along with a handful of fresh herbs and a few sprigs of parsley. Do not add salt. Cover the bird and vegetables with cold water, and bring to a boil over medium-high flame. Reduce the flame to medium-low, partially cover the pot, and simmer the bird until it is cooked through but not overdone. Generally, the bird should cook about 25 to 30 minutes per pound. Turn off the flame and remove the bird to a colander to drain and let stand 10 minutes. If you wish, transfer the chicken pieces to a casserole, pour a wonderful curry or tomato sauce over the chicken, cover, and bake in a 350-degree F oven for 15 minutes, and it's ready to serve.

Easy Steaks, Chops, and Pork Tenderloins

Busy cooks learn to be wizards with the small, convenient cuts of meat that can be defrosted, cooked in a flash, and jazzed up with quickly prepared condiments. The trick is to choose the right cuts, store them for fast defrosting, and get familiar with the basic cooking techniques that suit them best. Steaks, chops, and tenderloins are also great on the grill (see pages 160–61).

Juicy Beef Steaks in No Time Flat

If you love beef, you're in luck. It's available everywhere in lots of convenient cuts that you can freeze and defrost easily out of a standard refrigerator-freezer. For a big T-bone or Porterhouse you may want to fire up the grill (see pages 160–61). But for a scrumptious quick supper we prefer the small boneless steaks we can sauté or cook in a stove-top grill pan in nothing flat.

You can get exquisite steaks to order from your butcher, of course, for an exquisite price. Sometimes we indulge ourselves with filet mignon or New York strip steaks, but for everyday cooking we rely on pre-wrapped "economy packs" of boneless rib-eye steaks at our local grocery. We can get 6 to 8 nicely marbled little steaks for freezing at home, and the meat is both tender and flavorful. Our preference is for boneless steaks, 6 to 8 ounces each, cut ¾-inch thick. One steak per person is usually plenty—unless some of the persons are teenagers. These little steaks freeze and defrost quickly, and keep in the freezer for several months. Shop around until you find a beef supplier you can rely on to provide the quality you expect.

Make sure the steaks you buy have not been previously frozen. If they have, you should probably not re-freeze them, but rather cook them within a few days. If they're fresh, you can rewrap them separately at home for freezing. We dry them carefully; wrap each tightly in butcher's paper or plastic wrap; place them on the floor of the freezer, widely separated, until frozen; and then seal them into a heavy-duty freezer bag until they're needed.

Alternatively, we dry steaks thoroughly; coat them with a good dry rub or thick marinade; let them stand 30 minutes, covered, at room temperature; wrap each tightly in butcher's paper or plastic wrap; place them on the floor of the freezer, widely separated, until frozen; and seal them into a heavy-duty freezer bag. Be sure to label the freezer bag with the rub or marinade you've used so there won't be any surprises!

Freezing red meat before cooking has the advantage of tenderizing it somewhat by breaking down muscle fibers, but it has the disadvantage of releasing some of the meat's juices and allowing them to escape in the defrosting process. One way we combat moisture loss is to only partially thaw the meat before cooking.

To defrost a rib-eye steak, we pull it out of its freezer bag and seal it into a fresh one. Audrey gives it about 2 minutes on the microwave turntable at a "defrost" setting, and then lets it stand for 10 minutes before cooking. (You'll have to figure out the time and setting that works best for your own microwave.) Kathleen submerges the bag in a sink of lukewarm water for about 5 minutes, and then lets it stand 10 minutes. In either case, it is best not to completely defrost the meat. Just give it a good start so that the cooking process will finish the job and not leave you with a core of cold, raw flesh.

Partial defrosting will leave some of the moisture in the meat that would escape with complete defrosting, and we further minimize moisture loss by searing the meat at a high temperature to seal in juices. If you have marinated the steaks before freezing, wipe the marinade or rub off the steaks before proceeding to cook the meat.

We have two basic treatments for beef steaks: sautéing and stove-top grilling. Remove the semi-defrosted steaks from their wrappings, dry them thoroughly, and rub them with a little olive oil and salt and pepper if you wish.

Sautéed Steaks

Heat ½ tablespoon of olive oil and ½ tablespoon of butter in a heavy skillet over medium-high flame until the butter foams and is hot but not smoking. Put the steaks in the pan and cook quickly—2 or 3 minutes on each side for rare, and a little longer for medium rare. We think steak is done when little droplets of pink juice begin to emerge on the top (after it has been turned, of course). If you have any doubts, cut into the meat to see that it's done to your liking. Serve the steaks immediately with some grand sauce, salsa, slaw, or other condiment.

Stove-Top Grilled Steaks

Preheat a cast-iron or other heavy, ridged grill pan over medium-high flame until hot. Brush the ridges of the pan with a little olive oil and place the steaks over the ridges. Cook the steaks about 2 to 3 minutes on each side, until done to your liking. Serve the steaks immediately, with a great sauce.

Lamb, Pork, and Veal Chops

We love loin and rib chops, not least of all because we get to chew on those rich, delicious bones! If you prefer, you can also get boneless rib chops, which are like little rib-eye steaks. They cook a little faster, but we think you'll be missing a lot of great flavor. We never buy blade or shoulder chops. They tend to be tough, and they don't cook evenly.

For super-quick cooking, we want thin cuts that we can sauté, generally about ¾-inch thick. We plan on serving two per person. Thin-cut pork chops are easy to find in "economy packs." If they have not been previously frozen, we take them home and rewrap them for freezing, and then defrost them exactly the way we do steaks (see above). Avoid buying pork chops that are cut too thin, because pork chops can overcook and turn tough and dry.

Lamb and veal chops are another and quite luxurious matter, and we go to the butcher to order them specially cut. We sometimes freeze them as we do other chops and steaks, but we don't pull them out of the freezer unless some very special guests are showing up!

If you're cooking chops fresh, they can benefit from a rub or marinade at room temperature for 30 to 40 minutes before they're cooked.

Sautéed Chops

Defrost and pat dry 4 chops as you would a steak (see above). Rub them with a little salt and pepper if you wish, and some dried herbs. Heat 2 tablespoons of olive oil and 2 tablespoons of butter in a large, heavy skillet over medium flame until the butter foams and is hot but not smoking. Put the chops in the pan in a single layer and brown slowly, 4 to 5 minutes on each side, or until done. If you have any doubts, cut into the meat to see that it's done to your liking.

Monitor pork and veal chops carefully. If the chops cook too quickly or too long they will lose their juices and become tough. The days are gone when pork had to be cooked to the condition of shoe leather to guard against trichinosis! For lamb chops, which have more fat, you can use a little higher flame and not cook them quite so long, especially if you wish your lamb a little on the rare side. Remove the chops from the pan when the meat is still rosy and juicy, and serve them right away with a great sauce.

Stove-Top Grilled Chops

We think this treatment is great for lamb chops, but we don't recommend it for pork or veal, which may tend to dry out and get tough. Preheat a cast-iron or other heavy, ridged grill pan over medium-high flame until hot. Brush the ridges of the pan with a little olive oil and place the chops over the ridges. Cook the chops about 4 minutes on each side, until done to your liking. Serve the chops with a good sauce or salsa on the side.

Baked or Braised Chops

We also like thicker chops baked or braised, with or without stuffing. It gives us a little more time to get the rest of supper together, and a dish of oven-cooked chops will generally hold up beautifully if the meal is delayed a while.

For baking or braising, buy chops that are at least 1 inch thick; if you plan to stuff the chops, buy them 1½ inches thick, on the bone. Defrost and pat dry the chops as you would steaks (see above). Rub them with a little salt and pepper and dried herbs if you wish. Heat 2 tablespoons of olive oil and 2 tablespoons of butter in a large, heavy, oven-proof skillet over medium-high flame until the butter foams and is very hot but not burning. Put the chops in the pan in a single layer and brown quickly, about 2 minutes on each side, and cut off the flame.

For baking chops, preheat the oven to 400 degrees F. If you wish, cut a pocket horizontally in each browned chop from the rounded side to the bone, and stuff lightly with a mixture of seasoned bread crumbs and chopped onion, mushroom, parsley, and herbs bound with a little beaten egg. Stuffed or not, tilt the chops up against each other so they are not lying flat in the skillet, pour ¼ cup water or white wine into the skillet and place it in the hot oven. Bake the chops uncovered for 20 minutes, and then test for doneness. Continue baking to desired doneness, checking every 5 minutes. If the chops are stuffed, they may take a few minutes longer to cook through. If you have to hold dinner, turn off the oven and leave the door slightly ajar; cover the skillet and leave the chops in the oven until ready to serve.

To braise chops, preheat the oven to 350 degrees F. Melt ¼ of a stick of butter and pour it into a small skillet. Finely dice 1 carrot, 1 stalk of celery, and half of a white onion, and toss together with 2 tablespoons of fresh parsley leaves, chopped. Sauté the vegetables in butter over a medium flame until wilted, about 7 minutes. If you have a thick vegetable or chile sauce available, you can use the sauce instead of (or in addition to) the vegetables as a bed for braising the chops.

Spread half the vegetables or sauce into a glass or ceramic casserole with a lid, just large enough to hold the chops comfortably when they are tilted slightly against each other. Stuff the chops if you wish (see above), and arrange them on the vegetables or sauce. Spread the remaining vegetables or sauce over the chops, cover the casserole tightly, and put in the oven. Pull out the casserole and test a chop for doneness after 30 minutes—timing will depend not only on the thickness of the chops and whether they are stuffed or not but on the kind of casserole you're using. Return the dish to the oven, checking it every 5 minutes until done. Serve the chops immediately with a great salsa or dressing, or in their braising sauce. If you have to hold dinner, turn off the oven and leave the door slightly ajar, and leave the chops in the oven until ready to serve.

The Little Pork Tenderloin

We think succulent little pork tenderloins are a wonderful and versatile product and everybody should have one or two in the freezer. You can obtain pork tenderloins individually from your butcher, of course, but the widely available commercial brands are generally packaged in pairs. Typically, each tenderloin weighs about ¾ of a pound, making a substantial dinner for two (we think 6 ounces of meat at a sitting is as much as the average person can deal with).

Make sure the tenderloins you buy have not been previously frozen. If they have, you should probably not refreeze them, but rather should cook them within a few days. If they have not been frozen, we rewrap them separately at home for freezing. We dry them carefully; wrap each tightly in butcher's paper or plastic wrap; place them on the floor of the freezer, widely separated, until frozen; and then seal them into a heavy-duty freezer bag until they're needed. As with other cuts, we may let the tenderloins stand in a spicy rub for 30 minutes before freezing.

Freezing pork tenderloins before cooking has the advantage of tenderizing them somewhat by breaking down muscle fibers, but it has the disadvantage of releasing some of the meat juices and allowing them to escape in the defrosting process. One way we combat moisture loss is to only partially thaw the meat before cooking.

To defrost a tenderloin, we pull it out of its freezer bag and seal it into a fresh one. Audrey gives it 3 minutes on the microwave turntable at a "defrost" setting, then lets it stand 10 minutes. (You'll have to figure out the time and setting that works best for your own microwave.) Kathleen submerges the bag in a sink of lukewarm water for about 7 minutes, then lets it stand 10 minutes. In either case, it is not necessary to defrost the tenderloin completely. Just give it a good start so that the cooking process will finish the job and not leave you with a core of cold, raw flesh. Partial defrosting will leave some of the moisture in the meat that would escape with complete defrosting, and we further minimize moisture loss by searing the meat at a high temperature to seal in juices.

We have two basic treatments for the quick pork tenderloin supper: the stove-top sauté and the high-temperature roast. Both start with browning. Remove the semi-defrosted tenderloin from its wrappings, dry it thoroughly, and rub it with a little salt and pepper if you wish. In a heavy, oven-proof skillet, heat 2 tablespoons of olive oil until very hot but not smoking. Brown the tenderloin in the hot oil, turning with tongs as necessary to brown all sides of the meat and seal in the juices, which should take about 8 minutes.

Sautéed Pork Tenderloin

After browning (see above), remove the meat to a cutting board and let it stand untouched for about 10 minutes. Meanwhile, pour the scorched oil out of the skillet and wipe it clean. Put 2 tablespoons of fresh olive oil and 2 tablespoons of butter into the skillet. Heat the skillet over a medium flame until the butter has foamed and the skillet is hot. Using a very sharp knife, slice the tenderloin on a slight bias into medallions about ⅓-inch thick and place them in the skillet. Sauté the medallions, turning once, for a minute or two per side. Voila! Pour a wonderful sauce over the medallions, or serve them with a bright and spicy salsa or slaw on the side.

Roasted Pork Tenderloin

After the tenderloin has been browned, transfer it from the skillet to a preheated 400-degree F oven and let it dry roast for 12 to 15 minutes. Test for doneness by slicing into the meat or by inserting a meat thermometer. Internal temperature should be 165 to 170 degrees F. Remove the meat to a cutting board and let it stand about 10 minutes. Using a very sharp knife, slice the tenderloin on a slight bias into medallions about ⅓-inch thick, and serve them with a marvelous sauce, salsa, or slaw.

Simple Seafood

Never has there been such an abundance of seafood available, and nothing is simpler to cook or makes a healthier quick meal. For this book, we're confining our definition of "simple seafood" to commonly available fish, shrimp, and scallops. We think every freezer should be supplied with the household's favorites. If properly packaged and stored at no more than zero degrees, fish fillets, shrimp, and scallops can last up to six months without losing quality.

Here's our general rule: for supper tonight, buy fresh or previously frozen fish; for freezer storage, buy frozen fish—and take it home packed in a bag of ice! We have been known to buy very fresh fish fillets and then freeze them at home, but only if we're going to use them within a week or two. We don't recommend freezing fresh fish at home unless you have a powerful, sub-zero deep freezer.

Unless you live next to the seashore, much of the "fresh" seafood displayed on ice at your grocer's was shipped frozen and defrosted for sale. Almost all shrimp in U.S. markets, for example, is previously frozen. That is no mark against it! Fish which is flash-frozen immediately after harvest (e.g., on a factory ship at sea) and shipped frozen is likely to be "fresher" than the fish that spent three or four days traveling to market on ice without benefit of a deep freeze. We think it's unwise, however, to freeze fish that has already been frozen and defrosted once, so when we buy fresh or previously-frozen fish we cook it within 24 hours.

Follow your nose! Be as picky about your fishmonger as you are about your dinner guests. Buy from an establishment that is kept sparkling clean, that smells fresh and wonderful, and whose personnel can tell you more than you ever wanted to know about the provenance of each creature on display. Whole dressed fish should have clear, shiny eyes; bright, smooth scales; plump, red gill slits; and a fresh odor. Fresh or previously-frozen fillets and steaks should have moist, smooth flesh with no dull, dried, broken, or gummy appearance. Shrimp should have moist, pearly shells without breaks or black blotches. Shelled shrimp and scallops should have moist, firm flesh with no evidence of dryness.

Always ask your fishmonger about any item you're interested in the following questions: Where is it from? Was it shipped frozen, or is it fresh? Is it from northern waters or tropical waters? Is it caught wild, or farm-raised? The more you know about each piece of fish you buy and taste, the more knowledge you bring to your next selection. For example, farm-raised Atlantic salmon is available virtually everywhere these days at a reasonable price; but we think wild-caught silver salmon and king salmon from the Pacific Northwest is so much better that we're willing to pay the higher price for it when we can find it. Choosing the fish you really like is the key to enjoying it!

After we've made our selection, we always look it over carefully and give it the nose test before it's wrapped up—any whiff of ammonia or "fishy" smell, and we decline the purchase and shop elsewhere.

For the freezer, we buy frozen product, and keep it packed in ice all the way home to our kitchen freezer. If you have a good fishmonger, ask what he or she can do for you. He may be able to take your order for exactly the frozen seafood you want from exactly the right part of the world, and call you when it arrives. And you'll pay a premium price, of course. But there are good commercial brands of frozen fish fillets, fish steaks, shrimp, and scallops that won't cost an arm and a leg. Ask your fishmonger for advice about the best brands. Also, check the packaging of the product. If the package looks crushed or manhandled, or has a coating of ice anywhere on the outside, it may have been partially defrosted and then refrozen somewhere on its trip from the processing factory to the retailer. We wouldn't buy it. Try your locally available brands until you're satisfied that you've found the best, and then stick with them.

For quick suppers, we buy fresh or frozen fillets of lean, mild-flavored, white-fleshed fish such as cod, haddock, flatfish (sole, flounder, halibut, turbot), monkfish, tropical sea bass, grouper, red snapper, or orange roughy, planning on 6 to 8 ounces per person. Fillets can be sautéed, poached, baked, broiled, or braised. If we're buying fresh fish for immediate cooking, we like to buy a whole dressed fish; that means it has been cleaned, scaled, and de-finned, with the head and tail left on. Whole dressed trout, whitefish, striped bass, or red snapper are good choices when they're available. A 1½ to 2-pound dressed fish will serve two people nicely. We poach them to serve hot or cold, or stuff and bake them.

For baking, broiling, or grilling, we buy steaks of the firm and fat, dark-fleshed and strongly flavored fish such as salmon, swordfish, and (if we're feeling flush) tuna or mahi-mahi. We buy steaks cut no more than ¾ to 1 inch thick and weighing about 8 ounces.

We generally stick to jumbo or larger shrimp (20-24 to the pound) in the shell. We buy in the shell because we think they're likely to be fresher, the meat hasn't been handled, and we store the shells in the freezer for making shrimp stocks and shrimp butters. It's certainly a time saver to buy them already shelled, however.

Defrost frozen seafood slowly in the refrigerator if you can. If you put a 1-pound package of small fish fillets in the refrigerator before you go to bed, it should be ready to cook for dinner the next evening. If you forgot, you can seal the package of frozen seafood into a freezer bag and drop it into a basin of lukewarm water for half an hour, then open the package, separate the fillets and defrost at room temperature until free of ice. We don't recommend using a microwave oven to defrost seafood, because microwaving can so easily "cook" parts of the seafood and destroy the texture of the meat. Large fish fillets (more than a pound) or whole dressed fish should always be given the time necessary to defrost slowly and uniformly in the refrigerator. Unlike red meat, seafood should be completely defrosted before cooking.

Handle raw seafood the same way you handle raw poultry or other meat. Keep it well chilled until immediately before cooking. Store it tightly wrapped and separated from other foods. Always wash your hands, knives, cutting board, and other utensils and equipment in hot sudsy water after handling raw fish.

Seafood has a very high water content and cooks very fast. Always watch the dish closely and test for doneness sooner rather than later! It's easy to cook the dish another 2 minutes if it's not quite done, and quite impossible to salvage the results if it's overdone. When seafood is done, the flesh has turned from a soft, moist texture and pearly translucent appearance to a firm texture and opaque appearance. We follow the "Canadian rule" that a fish steak or fillet cooks through in 10 minutes for each inch of thickness. At high altitudes, poaching or braising takes a bit longer. Many fish fillets, however, are less than ½ inch thick, so be alert to how quickly the dish will be ready to serve!

Sautéing, poaching, baking, broiling, and braising are easy ways to produce a delicious seafood meal in a hurry. If you have the time and equipment, seafood is great on the grill, too (see pages 161–62). Although some folks cook fish in a microwave oven, we do not because the risk of overcooking is very high.

Small Fish Fillets, Shrimp, or Scallops for Two

Here's how to do a quick dinner for two with 1 pound of small fish fillets (no more than ½-inch to ¾-inch thick), jumbo shrimp, or sea scallops that are ½-inch to ¾-inch thick. Add a favorite salsa, sauce, or slaw and you're done!

Sautéed Seafood

If the seafood is frozen, defrost it and dry it thoroughly with paper towels. Shrimp may be cooked in their shells or peeled. Sprinkle the seafood with salt and pepper if you wish. You could dust fillets, scallops, and peeled shrimp lightly with flour if you want a little crispy crust on the seafood.

Heat 3 tablespoons of butter and 3 tablespoons of peanut oil in a large, heavy skillet (preferably non-stick) over a medium flame until the butter has foamed and the oil is hot, but not smoking. Carefully slide the seafood pieces into the skillet. Reduce the flame, if necessary, so that the oil is bubbling but in no danger of burning.

Sauté the seafood 2 or 3 minutes, then turn with a spatula. After another minute or two, remove a piece and test for doneness. When the flesh is cooked, remove immediately to paper towels to drain. This all happens very fast—take care not to overcook the seafood. Serve immediately with a great sauce or salsa.

Poached Small Fillets or Scallops

If the seafood is frozen, defrost it and separate the pieces. Put a high-sided skillet or sauté pan over a medium-high flame and pour in ½ cup dry white wine and 1 cup water. Add ¼ teaspoon salt, 2 peppercorns, several lemon slices, ¼ of a sliced onion, and a few sprigs of fresh parsley. Bring the liquid to a simmer, carefully lay in the fish fillets or scallops (adding more hot water, if necessary, to cover with liquid), cover the pan, and reduce the flame to keep the liquid at a bare simmer.

After 4 minutes, remove the lid, pick up a piece with a slotted spatula, and lift the piece onto a platter. Test the meat for doneness. If it still looks somewhat translucent, return it to the poaching liquid for another minute or two, then test again. The fish will cook faster at sea level than at high altitudes. When the seafood is done, remove to a platter (discarding the poaching liquid), surround with a spicy salsa or slaw, and serve.

Poached Shrimp

Defrost the shrimp, which can be poached in their shells or peeled. Put 3 quarts of water in a large pot and set over a high flame. Add 2 teaspoons of salt and a tablespoon of "shrimp boil" or pickling spices if you wish, and bring to a rolling boil. Scatter the shrimp into the pot and return to boil. The shrimp are done when the shells turn red, or the meat is firm, white, and opaque. At sea level, jumbo shrimp in the shell should be fully cooked within 2 or 3 minutes of going into the pot. It will take longer at higher altitudes because water boils at a much lower temperature. Remove the shrimp with a strainer, or empty the entire pot through a colander as soon as the shrimp are cooked. Plunge shrimp into ice water to chill for serving cold; otherwise, serve immediately with a great sauce or salsa.

Baked Seafood

If the seafood is frozen, defrost it and dry thoroughly with paper towels. Shrimp may be cooked in their shells or peeled. Preheat the oven to 400 degrees F. Melt ½ of a stick of butter and pour half of the melted butter into a glass or ceramic baking pan just large enough to hold the seafood comfortably in a single layer. Arrange the seafood in the pan and sprinkle with the juice of a large lemon wedge and with salt and pepper if you wish. Drizzle the remaining melted butter over the seafood. When the oven is hot, pop in the pan and cook until done without turning. Pull out the pan and test a piece for doneness after 5 minutes—it should be close. Return the pan to the oven for a minute or two if necessary. Serve immediately, with a great salsa or dressing.

Broiled Seafood

Broiling can be accomplished very quickly and yields sweet, juicy fish. It does require, however, that you have very good ventilation in your kitchen—or be prepared to live with the smell of broiled fish for a while.

If the seafood is frozen, defrost it and dry it thoroughly with paper towels. Shrimp may be cooked in their shells or peeled. Preheat the broiler. Melt ½ of a stick of butter and pour half of the melted butter into a shallow metal baking pan just large enough to hold the seafood comfortably in a single layer. Arrange the seafood in the pan and sprinkle with the juice of a large lemon wedge and with salt and pepper if you wish. Drizzle the remaining melted butter over the seafood. Slide the pan under the broiler so the seafood is about 4 inches from the element, and broil until done without turning. Pull out the pan and test a piece for doneness after 3 or 4 minutes—it should be close to finished, depending on the thickness of the fillets. Return the pan to the broiler for a minute or two if necessary. Serve immediately, with a great salsa or dressing.

Braised Seafood

If the seafood is frozen, defrost it. Thin fillets (such as sole) should be folded over to make little "packages" ½ to ¾-inch thick. Shrimp may be cooked in their shells or peeled. Preheat the oven to 325 degrees F. Melt ½ a stick of butter and pour half of it into a small skillet. Finely dice 1 carrot, 1 stalk of celery, and ½ a white onion and toss together with 2 tablespoons of fresh parsley leaves, chopped. Sauté the vegetables in butter over a medium flame until wilted, about 7 minutes. If you have a thick vegetable or chile sauce available, you can use the sauce instead of (or in addition to) the vegetables as a bed for braising the fish.

Spread half the vegetables or sauce into a glass or ceramic casserole with a lid, just large enough to hold the seafood comfortably in a single layer. Arrange the seafood on the vegetables or sauce, and sprinkle with salt and pepper if you wish, and the juice of a large lemon wedge. Spread the remaining vegetables or sauce over the seafood, cover the casserole tightly and put in the oven. Pull out the casserole and test a piece for doneness after 15 minutes—timing will depend not only on the thickness of the meat but on the kind of casserole you're using. If necessary, return the dish to the oven, checking it every 3 or 4 minutes until done. Serve the seafood and vegetables immediately in the braising sauce or with a great salsa or dressing.

Cooking Whole Dressed Fish, Large Fish Fillets, and Fish Steaks

Here's how to handle whole dressed fish, larger fish fillets (1 or more inches thick), and thick fish steaks. The basic methods are the same, of course, but the techniques are sometimes a little different because of the size and weight of the meat being cooked.

Sautéed Fish Steaks or Large Fish Fillets

Follow the directions for sautéing small fillets above, but do not coat the fish with flour. Do not crowd the steaks or fillets together. If you are cooking several pounds of fish, you may have to sauté them in two batches.

Sauté the fish 5 minutes, then turn with a spatula. After another 2 or 3 minutes, remove a piece and test for doneness. When the flesh is cooked, remove immediately to paper towels to drain. The total cooking time for steaks or fillets that are 1 inch thick should be about 10 minutes. Serve it immediately with a great sauce or salsa.

Poached Whole Dressed Fish or Thick Fillets

We poach whole trout, striped bass, red snapper, or small salmon up to about 2 pounds. They will fit into a deep-sided, covered 14-inch diameter skillet or sauté pan (with the tail sticking up under the lid), or if you have a fish-poaching rig you can use that. The fillet thickness of the fish should be about ½ inch to ¾ inch at the thickest part near the backbone. We use the same procedure to poach very large fillets, such as a fillet of salmon, sea bass, or grouper that is more than 1 inch thick and weighs more than a pound. When you buy a large fillet for poaching, it's best to buy it with the skin still intact. If the fish has been frozen, thaw it slowly and completely in the refrigerator.

Put the skillet over a medium-high flame and pour in 1 cup dry white wine and 2 cups water. Add ½ teaspoon salt, 3 peppercorns, several lemon slices, ½ of a sliced onion, and a few sprigs of fresh parsley. Bring the liquid to a simmer. Meanwhile, cut a length of four-ply cheesecloth that is 8 inches wider and 8 inches longer than the fish or fillet. Place the fish lengthwise on one long edge and roll the fish up in the cheesecloth so that it is completely enclosed. Tie kitchen twine around the long ends.

When the liquid in the skillet has reached the simmer, lift the fish into the pan and settle it gently into the liquid, folding the long ends of the cheesecloth back over the fish. Add hot water, if necessary, so the fish is just covered by liquid. Cover the skillet and reduce the heat to medium-low, or just enough flame to keep the liquid at a bare simmer. After 4 minutes, remove the lid, pick up the long ends of the cheesecloth with tongs and drape them over the sides of the pan. Working quickly, and wearing oven mitts or other protection for your hands, grasp the long ends of the cheesecloth and lift the fish out of the skillet, reversing it onto a platter. Grasp the long ends of the cheesecloth and lift the fish back into the poaching liquid, and then cover the skillet. Cook on the other side for another 3 or 4 minutes for a whole fish, or 5 minutes for a thick fillet.

After the fish has been poaching for10 minutes total, it should be nearly done. Again, remove the lid, pick up the long ends of the cheesecloth with tongs and drape them over the sides of the pan. Working quickly, and wearing oven mitts or other protection for your hands, grasp the long ends of the cheesecloth and lift the fish out of the skillet and onto the platter. Partially unwrap the fish, carefully peel back a strip of skin at the thickest part of the fillet and flake the meat deeply with a fork. The meat should be firm and white (pink in the case of salmon, of course) and should flake easily. If it still looks somewhat translucent, rewrap the fish and return it to the poaching liquid for another 2 minutes, and then test again. Remember that the whole process takes a little longer at high altitudes, because the poaching water simmers at a much lower temperature than at sea level.

When the fish is done, lift it onto the platter to cool to room temperature and discard the poaching liquid. Unwrap the cooled fish and discard the cheesecloth. Carefully peel off and discard the skin, decorate the fish if you wish, surround it with a spicy salsa or slaw, and serve it up.

Baked Whole Dressed Fish, Fish Steaks, or Large Fish Fillets

If the seafood is frozen, defrost it and dry it thoroughly with paper towels. Preheat the oven to 400 degrees F. Melt ½ of a stick of butter and pour half of the melted better into a glass or ceramic baking pan just large enough to hold the fish, steaks, or fillets comfortably in a single layer. Fill the cavity of a whole dressed fish with sliced onion, a lemon slice, and a sprig of parsley. Arrange the fish, steaks, or fillets in the pan and sprinkle with the juice of a large lemon wedge and with salt and pepper if you wish. Drizzle the remaining melted butter over the fish. When the oven is hot, pop in the pan and cook until done without turning. Pull out the pan and test a piece for doneness after 7 or 8 minutes—it should be close to finished. Return the pan to the oven for a minute or two if necessary. The total cooking time for steaks or fillets that are 1 inch thick should be about 10 minutes. Serve immediately with a great salsa or dressing.

Broiled Fish Steaks or Large Fillets

Broiling can be accomplished quickly and yields sweet, juicy fish. It does require, however, that you have very good ventilation in your kitchen—or be prepared to live with the smell of broiled fish for a while. All in all, we'd rather bake it, sauté it, or take it outside to the grill.

If the fish is frozen, defrost it and it dry thoroughly with paper towels. Preheat the broiler. Melt ½ of a stick of butter and pour half of the melted butter into a shallow metal baking pan just large enough to hold the steaks or fillets comfortably in a single layer. Arrange the fish, steaks, or fillets in the pan and sprinkle with the juice of a large lemon wedge and with salt and pepper if you wish. Drizzle the remaining melted butter over the seafood. Slide the pan under the broiler so that the seafood is about 4 inches from the element, and broil until done without turning. If there is smoke, or the pan juices begin to burn, pull out the pan and pour ¼ cup of water or white wine around the fish.

Test the fish for doneness after 7 minutes—it should be close to finished, depending on the thickness of the fillets. If any translucent appearance remains at the center of the meat, return the pan to the broiler until done. The total cooking time for steaks or fillets that are 1 inch thick should be about 10 minutes. Serve them immediately with a great salsa or dressing.

Braised Whole Dressed Fish, Steaks, or Large Fillets

If the seafood is frozen, defrost it. Follow the instructions above for braising small fillets, but plan to test the fish for doneness after 25 minutes instead of 15 minutes—timing will depend not only on the thickness of the meat but on the kind of casserole you're using. Return the dish to the oven, checking it every 3 or 4 minutes until done. Total cooking time for whole dressed fish, steaks, or fillets that are 1 inch thick should be a little more than 10 minutes, and slightly longer at higher altitudes. Serve the fish immediately in its braising sauce or with a great salsa or dressing.

Hot Off the Grill!

The American passion for grilling isn't limited to the summertime backyard barbecue anymore. The enticing aroma of fresh meats and vegetables sizzles all year long— not only in backyards, but also on apartment balconies as well as in the kitchen.

There is a range of grilling possibilities, from the electric hibachi on the kitchen counter to the gas-fired luxury model on wheels, complete with spit-roaster and warming ovens, to the good old covered kettle loaded up with charcoal. Whatever your preference, after a little practice you can turn out great meals with a minimum of time and effort.

Charcoal Grilling

If it's your favorite, more power to you! Personally, we find that cooking with charcoal takes too long on the front end, building up the fire and waiting for it to reach temperature (generally 30 minutes or more), and too long on the back end, cleaning up the mess! Charcoal is also the most expensive fuel source. We think it's great for big backyard parties or family gatherings about once a year, but not for everyday grilling.

Gas Grilling

We think it's easy and convenient, and we use our gas grills all year long. Audrey's is a covered, propane-fired unit that will preheat to any temperature she wants in about 5 minutes and be ready to go. We can use it open for brazier grilling, or covered for indirect heat. It involves no ashes, and very little cleanup. When buying a gas grill, look for one that has at least 12,000 BTUs of power. The more heating force the better.

Electric Grilling

For quick brazier grilling of steaks, chops, chicken breasts, fish steaks, and skewered meats or seafood, Kathleen maintains you can't beat an electric counter-top grill. They heat up fast; the drip pan and the porcelain-glazed stoneware base fit right into the sink (or even the dishwasher) for instant cleaning up; and they are easy to store and move around. It's also great to have the food you're cooking right up at counter level and in full light—so there's no mystery about when it's done. There are limits, however, to the kind of grilling you can do. Covered grilling by indirect heat is out. Also, on most counter-top grills the rack is fixed at about 4 inches above the heating elements, which can make it a problem to grill very thick steaks, large whole fish, or chicken halves if you need to cut down the temperature. Of course, you need to have a piece of open counter without shelves hanging over it, and you need plenty of ventilation.

Using Wood Chips

You can use aromatic wood chips to enhance the flavor of grilled foods if you're using a covered charcoal or gas grill to cook by indirect heat. We find that using wood chips for brazier grilling provides the chef a nice aroma around the grill, but doesn't do much for the flavor of the meat. Hardwood chips and blocks for grilling are widely available, including alder, apple, cherry, hickory, maple, oak, and mesquite. Generally, the first step is to soak the wood in water for 30 minutes or more. For a charcoal grill, strew the soaked chips over the coals when they are spotted with ash and ready for grilling, just before you bank up the coals and put the drip pan on the fire grate. For a gas grill, layer the soaked chips or blocks on the lava rock around the outside of the drip pan after the grill is preheated.

Handy Equipment

Whatever the grilling method, there are some handy tools to have available. Choose utensils with long handles (we prefer stainless steel with wood handles). At a minimum, you'll need tongs, a fork, a spatula, a basting brush, and a good pair of mitts. Depending on the menu, you can also use drip pans (shallow disposable heavy-duty foil pans) for indirect heat, bamboo or stainless steel skewers, hinged wire grill baskets for fish or vegetables, and a meat thermometer. Especially when cooking chicken, it's smart to keep a spray bottle of water handy to douse flame flare-ups.

Preparing the Grill

To start with, use a good wire cleaning brush on the fire grate and on the grill or cooking surface before you fire up (usually not necessary with the electric counter-top grill). Soak the wood chips, if you're using them. If using charcoal, load the grill and light the fire at least 30 minutes before you want to begin cooking. If you don't use self-starting briquets, you can use a fire chimney, a solid or liquid starter, or an electric starter to get the coals going. Alternatively, preheat the gas or electric grill for 5 to 10 minutes.

For indirect grilling over charcoal, when the briquets are lightly covered with ash and at their hottest (generally 30 minutes or so after lighting), bank up the coals on either side of the grill rack and scatter the soaked hardwood chips onto the coals if you're using them. Put a drip pan on the fire grate that is about the same size as the area of the grill rack that will be occupied by the food you are going to cook. For a gas grill, put down a drip pan after the grill is preheated, and layer soaked wood chips (if you're using them) on the lava rock around the drip pan.

When ready to cook, spray or brush the grilling rack with vegetable oil to help prevent sticking. Set the grill rack about 4 or 5 inches above the coals or lava rock for most grilling. If you're using an electric counter-top grill, you probably have a fixed setting for the grill rack about 4 inches above the heating elements.

Preparing the Food

Most meats and fish should be brought to room temperature before grilling. If you are using a marinade or rub to flavor the meat, marinate the meat for at least 30 minutes before you plan to cook it. We find that marinating for more than a couple of hours does little to improve the flavor. Always wipe off the marinade before cooking the meat.

If you are planning to partially cook vegetables or meats (chicken, for example) before finishing on the grill, be sure you've got it done ahead of time.

If you will use a glaze or barbecue sauce to "mop" the meat on the grill, have it prepared and warmed before you begin cooking the meat. Remember that any grilling glaze or sauce with sugar, tomato, or fruit juice in it is likely to burn over a hot fire. It's best to use glazes and sauces in the last 10 or 15 minutes of grilling, and to turn the meat frequently to keep the sugars from scorching. If you're cooking over a medium or low fire, there is less danger of blackening the glaze.

If you are using a hinged wire basket (to hold a large fillet of fish, for example), spray or brush the basket with vegetable oil to prevent sticking. If you are using bamboo skewers, be sure to soak them in cold water for at least 30 minutes before using, or you'll find the ends of your skewers in flames before the food is cooked.

Okay, ready? Before we start we like to make sure we have everything we need at our fingertips. This is supposed to be fun and easy!

Grilled Chicken

Always bring poultry to cool room temperature before grilling it. Wipe off any marinade you have used before putting pieces on the grill, and brush the chicken with a little olive oil.

Skinless, boneless chicken breast halves are quickly grilled on an open brazier over hot or medium-hot flame, generally 5 minutes per side or less. Watch them carefully! They have no skin to insulate the meat, and if they overcook they could turn dry and tough.

Chicken quarters and pieces should be grilled on an open brazier over medium-hot flame. Grill the pieces for 35 to 45 minutes, turning every 5 minutes. Brush the chicken with glaze or sauce for the last 15 minutes on the grill to avoid burning the skin. To test chicken for doneness, remove a piece of chicken from the grill and cut into the meat near the bone; if it is no longer pink the meat is done.

Chicken halves, too, should be cooked over medium-hot flame. Flatten the chicken by breaking the joints at the wing, thigh, and drumstick, and twisting the wing tips under the back. Grill halves for 50 to 60 minutes, turning every 5 minutes. Brush the chicken with glaze or sauce for the last 15 minutes on the grill to avoid burning the skin. To test for doneness, remove a piece from the grill and cut into the meat near the bone; if it is no longer pink the meat is done.

A whole chicken (3 or 4 pounds) cooks best over indirect heat on a covered grill when the fire is hot. Grill the bird breast-side down until browned, about an hour. Turn the chicken breast side up and cook until done, brushing with a glaze or sauce during the last 20 minutes of cooking. Total cooking time should be 20 to 25 minutes per pound. Your bird is cooked when the internal temperature reaches 185 degrees F, and the juices run clear when you pierce the meat deeply with a fork near the thigh joint.

Kathleen has no patience for 45 minutes of chicken turning. Accordingly, she either roasts the chicken in a hot oven and then finishes it on the grill; or grills the chicken and finishes it in the oven. To preroast chicken, preheat the oven to 450 degrees F. Oil the chicken pieces and arrange in a shallow roasting pan. Let the chicken roast for 30 minutes (while you do something else). Remove the chicken pieces directly to the hot grill, and commence turning them. Baste them with glaze or barbecue sauce if you wish, and cook until done, about 10 or 15 minutes. To oven finish, put the chicken pieces on the hot grill to sear, and cook them, turning them every 5 minutes, for about 15 minutes. Meanwhile, preheat the oven to 350 degrees F. Baste the chicken with glaze or barbecue sauce if you wish, then remove the pieces to a shallow roasting pan and pop them into the oven to finish cooking for 35 to 45 minutes (while you do something else).

Grilled Steaks and Chops

For quick grilling of chops and steaks, we stick to the most tender cuts of beef, veal, lamb, and pork, cut 1 inch thick. Steaks and chops should be grilled on an open brazier over a hot flame to sear the meat immediately and hold in precious juices. Turning chops and steaks several times during cooking will help keep them juicy and tender.

We think steak is done when pink juices begin to emerge on the top. If you have any doubts, cut into the meat to see that it's done to your liking. Very large steaks (more than 1½ inches thick) should be tested with a meat thermometer and removed from the grill slightly before registering the desired temperature. The meat will continue to cook for a few minutes as it stands.

For rib-eye, T-bone, Porterhouse, New York strip, or sirloin steaks cut 1 inch thick, plan on 10 to 14 minutes total grilling time over a hot flame for rare meat (140 degrees F internal temperature). Grill thicker cuts over slightly lower heat, and test with a meat thermometer. Plan on 18 to 20 minutes of grilling time for rare if the meat is cut 1½ inches thick, and up to 30 minutes for rare if the meat is cut 2 inches thick.

Lamb chops cut 1 inch thick will grill to medium rare (145 degrees F internal temperature) in 8 to 10 minutes over a hot flame. Pork chops and veal chops cut 1 inch thick take 12 to 14 minutes to cook through over a hot flame. For very thick chops, grill over a slightly lower flame and use a meat thermometer to test for doneness (145 degrees F for lamb, 165 to 170 degrees F for veal or pork).

Grilled Seafood

Fish should be grilled quickly on an open brazier over a hot flame. Firm-fleshed, fatty, deep-water fish (such as silver or king salmon, swordfish, tuna, or mahi-mahi) cut in 1 inch steaks can be cooked directly on the well-oiled grill rack without falling to pieces. Whole fish or fillets, however, should be enclosed in a hinged grill basket so they can be turned easily and will hold together. Shrimp and scallops can be skewered, or enclosed in a hinged grill basket. Use long stainless-steel skewers, flattened so that the meat doesn't just rotate on the skewer when you try to turn it; or use long bamboo skewers soaked in water for at least 30 minutes.

Enclose well-oiled whole dressed fish (up to 2 pounds) in a hinged grill basket and cook in a covered grill over indirect heat. The fire should be hot and the coals banked to either side of a drip pan directly under the fish. If you're using a gas grill, cover the lava stone area under the fish with a drip pan. Grill a 2-pound fish for 15 to 20 minutes total, turning once.

Put fish steaks cut 1 inch thick directly on the oiled grill rack over a hot flame, and turn once during cooking. Salmon will cook through in 6 or 7 minutes, up to 10 minutes for well-done fish. Swordfish and mahi-mahi will cook in about 8 minutes; tuna will cook to rare in 6 or 7 minutes, up to 12 minutes for very well-done fish.

Enclose fish fillets in a hinged grill basket and cook over a hot flame. Fillets no more than ½ to ¾ inches thick will grill in 5 to 8 minutes; turn them once during cooking and watch them carefully so as not to overcook. Fillets cut 1 inch thick will generally cook through in 10 minutes; turn them once during cooking.

Enclose shrimp or scallops in a well-oiled hinged grill basket, or thread on skewers. Grill on an open brazier over a hot flame. Jumbo shrimp generally cook through in about 5 minutes; large sea scallops may take 2 minutes more. Don't overcook!

Grilled Vegetables

Vegetables are vegetables…but grilled vegetables are something else! Most vegetables will grill to perfection in 8 to 12 minutes, on their own or snuggled up to your steaks or chops. We think if you're going to fire up the grill for meat, you may as well toss some wonderful vegetables on the brazier at the same time.

Well before grilling time, rinse, trim, and cut the vegetables into a uniform shape and thickness for the grill. The pieces should be flat if you are using a grill basket, or in cubes or chunks for threading on skewers. Pre-cook any vegetables that require it. Coat the vegetables in oil, or in a marinade or grilling glaze, before putting them on the grill. Grill vegetables on an open brazier over a medium-hot flame.

Artichokes, asparagus, carrots, beets, and potatoes should be steamed or cooked in boiling water until just tender before they go on the grill. Boil whole artichokes (see pages 11 and 12), and then cut them in half lengthwise to put on the grill, or trim out the whole heart and grill it. Steam asparagus until just tender (3 or 4 minutes, depending on size), line up whole stalks in the grill basket, and douse with oil. Trim carrots into uniform chunks, and beets, yams, or potatoes into uniform chunks, slices, or wedges. Cook them in boiling water until just tender, about 8 to 10 minutes, and drain. Toss the vegetables with oil or marinade and thread on skewers or enclose in a grill basket. Any of these pre-cooked vegetables will be grilled through and ready to serve in about 10 minutes.

Leeks, scallions, and onions of all kinds are great on the grill and require no pre-cooking. Trim roots and green tops off leeks, split lengthwise, and enclose in a wire basket. Trim roots and green tops off scallions and enclose in a wire basket. Red onions, white onions, and sweet onions can be peeled and cut in neat rounds ½ inch thick and laid carefully into a grill basket; or cut into halves (if they're small) or quarters and threaded on skewers. Douse the onions with oil before grilling. Leeks and scallions cook in 5 to 7 minutes; onion rounds or chunks can take 15 minutes or more.

Summer squash, eggplant, and portobello mushrooms are grill favorites that couldn't be easier. You can leave baby zucchini or pattypan squashes whole. Larger squashes and eggplant can be cut into ½-inch thick rounds or split lengthwise into quarters. Portobello mushrooms can be stemmed and grilled whole, or the caps cut into ½-inch thick slices. Brush the vegetables liberally with oil or marinade, enclose in a grill basket, and grill over hot coals for 10 to 15 minutes.

Bell peppers, fresh chiles, tomatoes, and corn are traditional summertime favorites, and may be the easiest of all to grill. Rinse whole peppers and chiles, dry them, and toss them on the grill for 5 to 10 minutes. Alternatively, you can seed the peppers and chiles, cut them into uniform chunks, toss them with oil, and thread them on skewers to grill. Husk the corn, drizzle with oil, and grill for about 20 minutes, turning every 5 minutes. Cut big beefsteak tomatoes in half and squeeze out seeds. Arrange in a grill basket, drizzle with oil, and grill for 8 to 10 minutes, turning once. Delicious!

The Quick-Fix Pantry

How many times have you enthusiastically launched yourself into a great-sounding new recipe only to be stopped dead in your tracks because you've run out of anchovies, or you're short on capers, or you used the last of the curry powder a month ago?

It's bound to happen once in a while, but we find that maintaining a well-stocked pantry really does save time and money—not to mention the risk of a ballistic stress attack 10 minutes before dinner is scheduled to be served!

Our "quick-fix pantry" includes the dry larder, the refrigerator, and the freezer. If we were to stock the pantry all at once from scratch, we'd have to get a second mortgage to foot the bill. We find, however, that once we've built up the pantry—one jar of precious herbs or one bottle of priceless vinegar at a time—it's relatively painless to keep it stocked.

If we think ahead, we can take advantage of sales, special offers, and unique opportunities to acquire new or replacement stock without paying premium prices, and without accepting a substitute for the product we really want because we *have* to have something and we *have* to have it now.

This is hardly an exhaustive list, and there are many more wonderful things out there that we love to have handy. But we think the items in this list are essentials!

Pantry Essentials List

Anchovies. We can't live without these salty little flat fillets packed in oil. We use them for salsas, sauces, salad dressings, in sandwiches, on appetizers—you name it. We never buy anchovy paste. We think it's made from the poorest quality anchovies, and our experience is that it dries out or goes off easily, and never has a great flavor anyway.

Asian condiments. Soy sauce is not enough anymore! Numerous wonderful condiments from the Pacific Rim are finding their way into U.S. supermarkets and kitchens. What you can't find at your local grocery you can probably pick up at a specialty market nearby. In addition to soy sauce, we like to keep the following on hand: Thai curry paste, Asian chile garlic paste, Asian chile oil, five-spice powder, wasabi powder (Japanese horseradish; mix it with a little water or soy sauce), miso (Japanese soybean paste for soups and dressings), Thai fish sauce or Vietnamese nuoc mam, hoisin sauce, sweet soy sauce (thick and molasses tasting), and sesame oil.

Beans, black-eyed peas, and chick peas. We keep a supply of our dried favorites, but when time is short we use canned or frozen. Find your favorite brands and stock them.

Chiles, chile powders, and chile purees. We keep lots of these on hand, fresh and cooked, in the refrigerator and freezer. See pages 176–79 for complete information.

Chutney. We keep several good chutneys, including Major Gray's, on hand as additions to sauces, marinades, and dips. Naturally, we love to have our own homemade chutneys and relishes on the shelf as well.

Coconut. We keep unsweetened shredded coconut in the freezer. It keeps for months if it's tightly wrapped and sealed in an airtight container; a little toasting brings it back to life. We also

keep a can of unsweetened coconut milk on the shelf to enrich
Thai sauces, or any pungent sauces for tropical fish (like grouper
and snapper).

Dairy products. We can't do without unsalted butter, and we like
to have light cream, sour cream, and yogurt in stock for quick
cold sauces and dressings. We also try to have a variety of
cheeses in the refrigerator. We always buy good cheese in large
chunks, but not cheese that has been sliced, crumbled, or grated.
We think the more handling and processing, the lower the
quality. And it's expensive to buy cheese that's already been
shredded—we'd rather spend the money on a higher grade of
cheese. If the cheese is wrapped in plastic, we discard the plastic,
wrap the cheese in a brown paper sack, and then seal it into an
airtight plastic storage bag. Cheese wrapped in plastic will begin
to mold rather quickly. Among the absolute essentials in our
refrigerator are a large chunk of good Parmesan (it doesn't have to
be the most expensive; we found one from Argentina that we love)
for shaving and grating, fontina, blue cheese (Gorgonzola,
preferably), feta cheese, Asiago cheese, and a large piece of
Gruyère, Emmenthaler, or Jarlsburg.

Freezer stock. We try to keep on hand the essentials that will
enable us to put a beautiful and delicious meal on the table
within an hour. It can be done! Our freezer is full of nuts (see
pages 179–83); homemade stocks and sauces; roasted peppers
and chiles, and chile purees (see pages 176–79); fresh ginger root
(cut in 1-inch pieces, wrap each tightly in plastic, store in an
airtight freezer bag); filled pasta; and steaks, chops, pork
tenderloins, and fish fillets.

Fruits, dried. We use a lot of them in sauces, salsas, and slaws,
including raisins, currants, figs, apricots, cherries, cranberries,
and blueberries. If we buy them boxed, we seal the boxes into
airtight storage bags. If they came wrapped in plastic or
cellophane, we pour them into brown paper sacks, then seal the
sacks into airtight storage bags. Keep them in a cool, dark

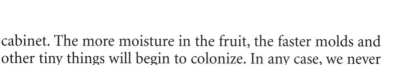
cabinet. The more moisture in the fruit, the faster molds and other tiny things will begin to colonize. In any case, we never keep dried fruits more than a few months.

Fruits, fresh. Lemons, limes, and oranges are on-hand essentials.

Herbs, dried. We keep a good stock of dried herbs. For many cooked dishes, dried herbs work just as well as fresh because the herbs are rehydrated and release their stored oils and flavors when heated. When substituting dried herbs for fresh herbs called for in the recipe for a cooked sauce or salsa, you should generally use about half the quantity of dried herb because it is more potent. However, we never substitute a dried herb when a fresh herb is called for in an uncooked sauce, salsa, or dressing. We buy dried herbs in small quantities because they are expensive and they don't retain their peak aroma and flavor forever. We always store dried herbs in airtight containers away from heat and light—never out on a decorative display rack where they look nifty but soon become worthless for cooking. We try to replace dried herbs that we've had hanging around for more than a year. Our most-used basics are basil, bay leaves, chervil, dill, marjoram, oregano, rosemary, sage, tarragon, and thyme.

Herbs, fresh. We keep fresh cilantro and parsley at all times. They keep well if you stand their stems in a glass of water and drop a plastic bag over the top. We grow some of our own herbs in pots, because they really have so much more flavor than the grotesquely expensive little plastic bags of herbs at the grocery. Favorites for pots are basil (a couple of varieties), oregano, thyme, and chives.

Honey. Volumes have been written about honey and its wonders. We use it in coffee and tea instead of sugar, and have used honey as a sweetening agent in lots of the recipes in this book. We prefer a dark, heavy honey. Our preference is Crockett's, an unfiltered raw honey produced in Arizona, which may not be available everywhere. Local and regional producers sometimes offer the best value for the dollar.

Horseradish. We like it fresh and grated at home, but the roots are not always available. So we keep bottled grated horseradish in the refrigerator.

Hot pepper sauce. We like our own (see page 42), but we always keep some on hand, including Tabasco, a chipotle hot sauce, and a green habanero hot sauce from the Yucatán.

Ketchup. We think this is basically awful stuff, full of sugar and salt. It inevitably reminds us of the greasy burgers and fries of our youth. We keep it around, though, because it's an essential ingredient in some of our favorite old-fashioned barbecue sauces.

Lard. Audrey won't touch the stuff, but Kathleen keeps some in the freezer. She uses it to make tortillas and pie shells, and it's also an ingredient of some good Mexican red sauces and Southern barbecue sauces.

Mayonnaise. When we're out of our own (see page 67 for making yours), we reach for the Hellman's.

Mustards. We keep both dry (Coleman's and Chinese) and prepared mustards. Prepared Dijon-style mustard is our kitchen standby, and we keep a more rustic grainy mustard, and a sweet brown mustard as well. There are a million mustards, so you have a lot of choices.

Nuts. We love nuts and buy lots in the fall and early winter to store away. Generally, we shell them and pack them into the freezer (see pages 179–80). Most used nuts are almonds, walnuts, piñons, pistachios, pecans, filberts, and peanuts.

Oils. For a run-down on the essential kitchen oils, see pages 172-74. We stock extra virgin olive oil, olive oil, canola oil, safflower oil, peanut oil, walnut oil, sesame oil, and Asian hot chile oil.

Olives. We love olives. Generally, we want brine-cured or oil-cured olives from a good Italian or Greek delicatessen. But we keep a stock of bottled or canned olives in the pantry for emergencies, including big Spanish green olives stuffed with pimiento; and brine-cured Kalamata or other Greek black olives. We don't buy the American black olives available everywhere in cans, because we regard them as totally without flavor. We want olives that sing!

Pasta, dried and filled. We keep lots of De Cecco dried pasta on hand, and our own filled pastas in the freezer when we can. Pasta is great for quick meals (see pages 126–30 for pasta basics).

Pickles. We keep lots of pickles on the shelf or in the refrigerator, including pickled capers (tiny and large sizes), cornichons (or tiny sour gherkins), sweet gherkins, pickled sweet peppers, and crunchy pickled onions.

Roasted red peppers. We roast, peel, and freeze our own peppers and chiles, but sometimes we use them up so fast we run out. It's good to keep a couple of jars of a good brand of roasted peppers packed in oil.

Salt. Our preference is for natural sea salt, which is available finely granulated or in "rocks" for grinding to your preferred coarseness. There is some difference from brand to brand in the actual sharpness or "saltiness" of the product, so shop for the one that suits you. Most sea salt is readily interchangeable with American iodized table salt, but it is sharper in flavor than kosher salt. For recipes in this book, we have tried to avoid specifying an amount of salt, particularly for uncooked sauces and dressings, and urge you to follow your own taste. For health reasons as well, we think it's better to start with less salt, and only add salt as necessary.

Seeds. Seeds are potent little packages of flavor just waiting to explode. To get the very most out of seeds, it's almost always a good idea to toast them lightly in a small, heavy skillet over a medium flame for just a minute or two, then pour them into a small mortar and lightly crush them with a pestle. Seeds are not only wonderful for baking but also for use in many sauces, dressings, marinades, and slaws. We buy and store them the same way we do dried herbs, but they last longer. We don't find it necessary to toss out unused seeds unless we've had them over two years. We always keep the following basics on hand: anise, caraway, celery, cumin, coriander, dill, fennel, mustard, peppercorns (black, pink, and green), poppy, and sesame.

Spices. We never use a lot of any of these powerful flavors, but when you need one of them there is often no substitute. Ground spices are often preferable to the whole spice, particularly for uncooked dishes. As with dried herbs, we store ground spices in airtight containers away from heat and light—never out on a decorative display rack, where they look great but soon become worthless for cooking. We try to replace the ones that we've had hanging around for more than a year. We always keep these basics on hand: cardamom powder, cayenne powder, cinnamon (whole and ground), cloves (whole and ground), curry powder, chile powders (see page 178), ground ginger, Chinese mustard, Coleman's mustard, nutmegs (whole), sweet paprika, vanilla (beans and extract).

Stock. We prefer to make our own chicken, beef, fish, and vegetable stocks and freeze them in small quantities to use in soups and sauces, especially cream sauces. We find that the canned stocks have a canned taste, and cubes or grains dissolved in water are too salty.

Sugar. We stock raw sugar or turbinado, when we can get it, and use it instead of refined white sugar for all our cooking. It takes a little longer to dissolve in liquids and is not as sweet as refined sugar, but we find it performs identically in every other respect. When you shop for raw sugar, read labels carefully. Some of what's on the market is actually refined white sugar with a pale brown coating bonded to the crystals. If you're paying for raw sugar, you ought to be sure you're getting it! In this book, almost every recipe that calls for sugar specifies raw sugar. If you are substituting refined sugar, remember that the dish will be sweeter unless you reduce the amount of sugar. We keep brown sugar on hand as an essential flavoring agent in many sauces, particularly for barbecue! American brown sugar is actually refined white sugar with some molasses added back in for color and flavor. If you're a purist, you might want to experiment with raw sugar and molasses as a substitute when a recipe calls for brown sugar.

Tahini. Sesame paste is a great condiment to have on hand. We use it in salad dressings and to make dips.

Tomatoes. These days, you can buy good Roma tomatoes (the red, thick pulp is the very best for making sauces) almost all year around. But when we can't, we rely on canned Italian plum tomatoes (whole, peeled) and a good brand of tomato paste. We rarely use them, but we're glad to know they are on the shelf.

Tuna, canned. Kathleen has to have tuna on hand to make *Tuna Caper Dressing* (see page 72). She puts it on cold shrimp, cold meats, deviled eggs, fresh vegetables, pita crisps, whatever. If no one's looking, she eats it with a spoon.

Vegetables, fresh. We're lost without a supply of fresh red onions, garlic, scallions, Roma tomatoes, chiles, bell peppers, mushrooms, and ginger.

Vinegars. For the low-down on essential kitchen vinegars, see pages 172–75. We stock white wine vinegar, champagne vinegar, red wine vinegar, apple cider vinegar, aged balsamic vinegar, sherry vinegar, rice vinegar, and raspberry vinegar.

Water chestnuts. We always have a few cans on the shelf. For crunch!

Wines and spirits. The kitchen stock of wines and spirits can be simple or vast, depending on your approach to cooking. An infusion of wine or brandy can turn some ordinary sauces into nectar of the gods! Still, we do not use much wine in cooking, and we prefer to keep a simple stock. We follow the age-old rule of quality and flavor: if we wouldn't serve it to guests at our table, we don't cook with it. Our essentials are a light, dry white wine, such as fume blanc; a full-bodied red wine, like pinot noir; a dry sherry; a Marsala or Madeira; a brandy; and an orange liqueur, such as Grand Marnier.

Worcestershire sauce. You may have another favorite, but this one is a staple for us. It goes into soups, sauces, salsas, dressings, and marinades.

Oil and Vinegar, Please!

Remember when vegetable oil was vegetable oil. . .tasteless, odorless, colorless, all-purpose national brands from frying pan to salad bowl? When vinegar was distilled white or cider, and that was about it?

Today the profusion of different and distinctive oils and vinegars displayed in confusing array on the grocery shelves can be daunting. But we think it's worthwhile to investigate as many as possible, particularly naturally flavored oils and vinegars from small manufacturers both here and abroad; they can spark up a dull dish with special verve, and serve as inspiration for creating your own flavored oils and vinegars very economically.

It is not necessary to pay a fortune for good oils and vinegars, but it should be no surprise that the best products tend to be more expensive. Never forget, however, that some of the worst products in the fad-ridden market of designer foods may also be among the most expensive. Caveat emptor! In the final analysis, you have only your own taste to rely on. You can experiment without buying if you stay alert to opportunities—if you love the salad dressing, ask your hostess or waitress what

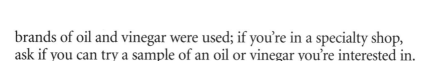
brands of oil and vinegar were used; if you're in a specialty shop, ask if you can try a sample of an oil or vinegar you're interested in.

When buying oils, try to choose a specific oil (e.g., corn oil, peanut oil, etc.) over a "vegetable oil" mixture; and, whenever possible, choose cold-pressed oils over oils extracted by heat or a chemical process. When buying flavored oils and vinegars, always read the label to learn what base oil or vinegar you're buying. When you pay $15 for a shapely bottle of vinegar with pretty fruit floating around in it and a cutesy raffia bow around the neck, remember that you may be investing more in the packaging than in the contents of the bottle!

We buy both oils and vinegars in small quantities, particularly flavored products that we may use infrequently. We store them in a dark, cool place and try to use them within a year. Oils continually exposed to light and heat in the kitchen will quickly turn rancid. Nut oils are particularly unstable; keep them in the refrigerator. Vinegars are sensitive to light as well, and may turn cloudy and bitter if not stored properly.

All-purpose vegetable oils. Any neutral, medium-weight oil of good quality can be used to bind vinegar, herbs, and spices into a glossy emulsion for dressing fresh fruits, vegetables, and greens. Our preference for most dressings is canola oil or safflower oil, with good binding performance and almost no flavor. Oils pressed from corn, sunflower seeds, peanuts, or soybeans work well too.

Olive oils. Olive oil may be light and delicate or fruity and robust, and we frequently use it when we want the oil to serve as a flavoring agent as well as a binding agent. In general, we find olive oil is more suited to vegetables and greens than to fruits. Extra virgin olive oil is the thick, dark green, highly fragrant, and flavorful first cold pressing from top quality olives. We hoard it like misers. Virgin olive oil is also fragrant and flavorful, but not as dominating as extra virgin, so it is generally more suitable for salad and salsa dressings. Olive oil that is not designated virgin or extra virgin may have mild flavor, or may be comparable to the all-purpose vegetable oils with virtually no flavor or odor. In most markets, you can buy olive oils from Italy, Greece, Spain, or France as well as from the United States, and you simply have to try lots of oils to find the ones you like best.

Flavored oils. In combination with neutral oils, we sometimes use small quantities of flavored oils with dramatic effects. Sesame oil, pressed from sesame seeds, is available in a light or dark concentration and has a very strong nutty flavor. It gives a characteristically Asian flavor to dressings and is good with both fruits and vegetables. Almond, filbert, macadamia, and walnut oils generally have a mild and delicious flavor and the aroma of the nut from which they're made, although we've come across some nut oils that have little more flavor or aroma than a neutral vegetable oil. Choose nut oils very carefully for the flavor and aroma you want; buy in small quantities and always keep them in the refrigerator. Garlic oils and chile oils are vegetable or olive oils that have been infused with garlic or chile flavor. Read labels carefully before you buy so you know what the basic oil is, and don't expect one brand to remotely approximate any other brand of the same product for intensity of flavor or aroma. We prefer to make garlic and chile oils at home so we know exactly what's going into the bottle; but there are some good infused oils out there, so give them a try.

Wine vinegars. We think every pantry should have a strong red wine vinegar (5 to 6 percent acetic acid), a mild white wine or champagne vinegar (4 to 5 percent acetic acid), and an aged Italian balsamic vinegar—all derived from grapes. The red will stand up well to other strong flavors such as chiles, mustards, and strongly flavored greens. Champagne vinegar is more delicate in flavor and not quite as harsh as white wine vinegar, and does well with fruits and with mildly flavored herbs. Aged balsamic vinegar is nectar from heaven, slightly sweet and very aromatic. As far as we're concerned, it goes with virtually everything. Aged balsamic vinegar is very expensive, and the older it is the higher the price. We also keep Spanish sherry vinegar handy; it is dark, rich, very potent and goes a long way.

Rice vinegar. Rice vinegar is fermented from rice but can also be made from rice wine, and you may see both kinds in your local specialty shops. It is a mild and delicately flavored vinegar (about 4 percent acetic acid) and can be used interchangeably with champagne vinegar.

Fruit vinegars. Our most familiar fruit vinegar is apple cider vinegar, but you also may be able to find vinegars fermented from other fruits, including pears, apricots, cherries, and pineapple. These vinegars should have the flavor and aroma of the fruits from which they're made, but intensity may vary a lot by brand. Fruit vinegars are great with fresh fruits and greens, of course, and may also be excellent additions to sauces for roast turkey, duck, or pork. Many popular fruit vinegars on the market (e.g., raspberry, blackberry, mango) are not actually made from the fruits used to flavor them. Instead, the fruit is mashed and steeped in vinegar (preferably red or white wine vinegar) until it has absorbed the flavor and aroma from the fruit. Again, the intensity of the flavor and aroma may vary significantly from one brand to another. You can also make your own fruit vinegar by steeping crushed fresh fruit (and perhaps a little sugar and spices) in a vinegar of your choice until you have the flavor and aroma you want.

Herb vinegars. Vinegars flavored with garlic, chiles, and various herbs are becoming more and more popular. As with most fruit vinegars, the flavoring agent is generally steeped in vinegar to impart its flavor and aroma. Both the quality of the vinegar used as the base and the intensity of the flavoring may vary considerably by brand, so the only way to discover the really good ones is to keep trying different brands. If you want to take the trouble, you can always make your own more economically.

The Chile Primer

The array of hot sauces, salsas, pickled and preserved chiles, and chile powders available in supermarkets today is astounding! But preparing your own fresh and dried chile concoctions "from scratch" is both simple and fun.

Roasting Fresh Chiles and Bell Peppers

At the market select firm chiles that are heavy and have a fresh smell. The skins should be dry, shiny, and smooth, without pits or blemishes that could indicate rot and without any signs of shriveling. You may be able to store fresh chiles in a paper sack for up to a week before using them. If your kitchen conditions are warm and damp, however, stash your chiles in the refrigerator. Use fresh chiles in three to five days, or roast and freeze them while they are still in top condition.

Our Favorite Fresh Green Chiles

Poblano is a mild to medium-hot dark green chile, 3 inches wide at "the shoulders" and 4 to 5 inches long, tapering to a point. *Jalapeño* is medium-hot with a fresh, crisp flavor, 1½ inches at the top and about 2 to 3 inches long, tapering slightly to a rounded bottom, and it is also widely available pickled *en escabeche*. *Serrano* is hot to very hot with a crisp, clear flavor, nearly cylindrical, ½ inch wide at the stem, about 2 inches long, and also widely available pickled en escabeche. *New Mexico green* is medium-hot to hot with a rich vegetable flavor, 2 inches wide at the top, and 6 to 8 inches long, tapering to a point. It is not widely available outside the Southwest except canned or frozen. *Anaheim* is a milder substitute for the New Mexico green chile, and it looks identical.

Skins of fresh chiles and bell peppers are the most indigestible part when cooked, and they should generally be charred and removed unless the chiles are to be used raw. The charring process will release strong fumes that can cause sneezing and stinging eyes—so be certain you have good ventilation.

CAUTION

Wear plastic gloves or wash your hands thoroughly as soon as you're finished. Never touch eyes, nose, or face after working with chiles until you have removed all traces of capsaicin from your hands.

Roasting chiles over a hot, open flame is the best method for charring them. Set a small, sturdy grill rack directly over the full-blast gas flame of the kitchen range. When the rack is hot, place the chiles on the rack and let them roast, turning with tongs to blacken them evenly (about 10 minutes overall). If you have an electric range, you can set the rack directly over the heating element. If you prefer to use the oven broiler, preheat it, and place the chiles on the broiler rack 1 or 2 inches below the flame or heating element, and then turn them with tongs until they are charred. Leave the broiler door open or the buildup of heat inside the oven will overcook the chiles.

Remove the charred chiles to a plastic bag and let them "sweat" for 10 or 15 minutes, or until they are cool enough to handle. The skins will then pull off fairly easily, depending on the type of chile. To store for later use, lay out the charred chiles on a baking sheet in their skins and freeze them, and then seal them into plastic freezer bags for storage so you can pull them out individually as needed. After the chiles are thawed, the skins slip off easily.

Dried Chiles, Powders, and Purees

Dried red chiles are available in the form of whole pods, pods crushed into flakes (chile Caribe), or pure powder. Whole dried chile pods are best when still slightly flexible and aromatic. Buy chiles that are whole, clean, uniform in color, and close to the same size. Reject chiles that are broken, faded or spotted, dusty or dirty, or show any evidence of insect infestation. Store dried chiles in airtight containers in a cool, dry place away from light. When buying powders, select pure chile powders—not "chili" seasoning powders that usually contain a variety of other spices and ingredients, from dehydrated garlic powder to sugar and artificial colorings. Buy slightly lumpy powder, an indication that the natural oils have not evaporated, and store it in an airtight container in a cool, dark, dry place or in the freezer.

Our Favorite Red Chiles

Ancho and **mulato** are dried poblano chiles, very dark mahogany color and wrinkled, about 3 inches at "the shoulders," 4 inches long, mild to medium heat, and with a rich, sweet flavor. *Pasilla* is the dried chilaca chile with an almost black, very wrinkled skin; about 1 inch wide at the stem and 5 to 6 inches long; mild to medium heat; and with a rich, slightly smoky flavor. *New Mexico red* is a deep, ruby red color with smooth, shiny skin; 1½ inches wide and 5 to 6 inches long; with an earthy sweet flavor; with medium to medium-high heat. *Chile colorado* is a dried Anaheim chile; bright fire-engine red with smooth, shiny skin; about 1 inch wide at the stem and 5 to 6 inches long; mild heat; and a substitute for New Mexico red chile. *Chipotle* is a smoked, dried jalapeño chile, very hot, with a distinctive smoked flavor; dull tan to coffee brown color; very shriveled appearance; 2 inches long and 1 inch across. Canned or bottled chipotles *en adobo* (that is, chipotles that have been rehydrated and pickled in a tomato-based sauce) are the most convenient form of chipotle for most cooking.

Dried red chile pods must be cleaned, rehydrated, and cooked before we can enjoy them in our food. In a hectic world, we find it convenient to reach into the refrigerator or freezer for chile puree we have already prepared. Generally, we get up to 1 tablespoon of thick puree per large chile pod.

To make puree, wipe the chiles with a damp cloth, break the stems off the chiles, and shake out the seeds. Scatter the chiles into a dry skillet over medium-high heat and dry roast them for 2 or 3 minutes, stirring or turning the pieces so they will not scorch. Put the chiles in a bowl, pour boiling water over them just to cover, and soak for 20 minutes or until soft. Spoon the chiles into a blender jar. Taste the soaking liquid—if it is very bitter, throw it out; otherwise reserve it. Pulse the chiles to a puree, adding soaking water (or fresh water) as needed to make a thick puree.

You can refrigerate the puree for several months in a clean glass jar with a thick film of olive oil floated over the top. For longer storage, measure the puree into an oiled ice cube tray, freeze, then pop the cubes into a freezer bag.

We're Nuts About Nuts!

From the lowly peanut (not technically a "nut") to the priceless piñon (if you've ever tried to shell one, you know why they're so costly), we love the aroma and flavor and richness and crunch of nuts!

At harvest in the fall, the grocery stores are full of fresh nuts, and we're accustomed to baking them into holiday cookies, cakes, and pies. But nuts are also grand additions to salsas, sauces, and slaws—not to mention soups and stews— throughout the year. If you find it painful (as we do) to hand over vast amounts of cash for those tiny cellophane bags of tired nuts in the baking aisle, stock up on fresh nuts in the fall and freeze them. Buy only a small quantity at first, and check to see that they really are fresh. If you find a significant number of rancid, dried, or wormy nuts, shop elsewhere for your supply. Spend a few evenings shelling (or put the kids to work on it), and then pack small quantities of whole nutmeats tightly in plastic bags and freeze them until you need them.

Frozen or not, all nuts benefit enormously from a light toasting or roasting to release their aromatic oils and enhance flavor. To roast: preheat the oven to 300 degrees F; spread the nuts in a roasting pan large enough to give them plenty of room in a single layer, and roast about 15 minutes, checking and stirring frequently to prevent scorching. To toast: preheat a heavy skillet over low to medium flame; spread the nuts in the skillet in one layer; toast, stirring constantly for 5 to 7 minutes; pour them out of the skillet to cool as soon as they begin to color.

To remove skins from almonds or pistachios, blanch them in boiling water for 3 or 4 minutes, run cold water over them, and slip the skins off with your fingers while the nuts are still damp.To remove skins from hazelnuts, roast them in a 275-degree F oven for 20 to 30 minutes, and then rub the skins off with a dish towel.

Most nuts take to herbs and spices with tantilizing results, and flavored nuts are great to have on hand for many uses. In an airtight container, they keep well for months in the freezer. Five minutes in a 300-degree F oven will bring the nuts back to just-roasted flavor and freshness. Use them extravagantly! They're good for you!

Hot Chile Nuts

2 cups nuts
1 tablespoon canola oil
½ teaspoon salt
1 teaspoon coriander seeds, toasted
1 teaspoon cumin seeds, toasted
2 teaspoons red chile powder

Preheat the oven to 300 degrees F. Sprinkle the oil over the nuts in a mixing bowl. Crush the salt, seeds, and chile powder together in a small mortar and sprinkle over the nuts. Toss the nuts to coat evenly with seasoning and spread them in a roasting pan in one layer. Roast 15 to 20 minutes, checking and stirring frequently to prevent scorching. Cool and store in an airtight container. *Yield: 2 cups.*

Curried Nuts

2 cups nuts
1 tablespoon canola oil
½ teaspoon salt
1 teaspoon coriander seeds, toasted
½ garlic clove, mashed
2 teaspoons curry powder

Preheat the oven to 300 degrees F. Sprinkle the oil over the nuts in a mixing bowl. Crush the salt, seeds, garlic, and curry powder together in a small mortar and sprinkle over the nuts. Toss the nuts to coat evenly with seasoning and spread them in a roasting pan in a single layer. Roast 15 to 20 minutes, checking and stirring frequently to prevent scorching. Cool and store in an airtight container. *Yield: 2 cups.*

Herbed Nuts

2 cups nuts
1 tablespoon canola oil
½ teaspoon salt
½ garlic clove, mashed
1½ teaspoons dried rosemary
¼ teaspoon dried thyme
¼ teaspoon dried parsley

Preheat the oven to 300 degrees F. Sprinkle the oil over the nuts in a mixing bowl. Crush the salt, garlic, and herbs together in a small mortar and sprinkle over the nuts. Toss the nuts to coat evenly with seasoning and spread them in a roasting pan in a single layer. Roast 15 to 20 minutes, checking and stirring frequently to prevent scorching. Cool and store in an airtight container. *Yield: 2 cups.*

Winter Spiced Nuts

2 cups nuts
1 tablespoon canola oil
⅛ teaspoon salt
⅛ teaspoon ground cloves
1 teaspoon ground cinnamon
1 pinch nutmeg
1 teaspoon raw sugar

Preheat the oven to 300 degrees F. Sprinkle the oil over the nuts in a mixing bowl. Crush the salt, spices, and sugar together in a small mortar and sprinkle over the nuts. Toss the nuts to coat evenly with spices and spread them in a roasting pan in a single layer. Roast 15 to 20 minutes, checking and stirring frequently to prevent scorching. Cool and store in an airtight container. *Yield: 2 cups.*

Ginger Soy Nuts

2 cups nuts
1 tablespoon canola oil
1 garlic clove, crushed
½ teaspoon ground ginger
1 tablespoon dark soy sauce

Preheat the oven to 300 degrees F. Sprinkle the oil over the nuts in a mixing bowl. Crush the garlic, ginger, and soy sauce together in a small mortar and sprinkle over the nuts. Toss the nuts to coat evenly with seasoning and spread them in a roasting pan in a single layer. Roast 15 to 20 minutes, checking and stirring frequently to prevent scorching. Cool and store in an airtight container. *Yield: 2 cups.*

Honey Roasted Nuts

2 cups nuts
¼ cup honey
½ teaspoon salt
1 to 2 teaspoons spices (optional)

Preheat the oven to 300 degrees F. In a small saucepan over medium flame, heat the honey with salt (and spices if desired, e.g., chile powder, curry powder, ground cinnamon, and cloves) and stir until the honey is liquefied. Let cool to warm room temperature. Put nuts in a deep bowl, drizzle with honey mixture and stir to coat nuts. Oil a roasting pan and spread nuts into the pan in a single layer. Roast for 10 minutes, checking and stirring frequently to prevent scorching. Cool and store in an airtight container. *Yield: 2 cups.*

Index

Where to Buy Chiles

The chile products used in these recipes are widely available in supermarkets and specialty stores in major metropolitan areas around the country. If you have difficulty finding chiles in your locality, call one of these reliable sources. Many of them provide regular mail order services.

SOUTHWEST

Bueno Foods
2001 4th Street SW
Albuquerque, NM 87102
505-243-2722
1-800-95CHILE
www.buenofoods.com

Casados Farms
Box 852
San Juan Pueblo, NM 87566
505-852-2433

Chile Addict
325 Eubank NE
Albuquerque, NM 87123
505-237-9070
www.chileaddictstore.com

Chile Hill Emporium
P.O. Box 685
Placitas, NM 87043
505-867-3294

The Chile Shop
109 East Water Street
Santa Fe, NM 87501
505-983-6080
www.thechileshop.com

Chile Traditions
8204 Montgomery Blvd. NE
Albuquerque, NM 87109
505-888-3166
1-877-VERY-HOT
www.chiletraditions.com

Los Chileros
401 2nd. St. S.W.
Albuquerque, NM 87102
505-768-1100
1-888-328-2445
www.888eatchile.com

Chili Pepper Emporium
901 Rio Grande NW
Suite A-194
Albuquerque, NM 87104
505-881-9225
1-800-288-9648
www.chilipepperemporium.com

Da Gift Basket
P.O. Box 2085
Los Lunas, NM 87031
505-865-3645
1-877-468-2444
www.dagiftbasket.com

Hatch Chile Express
P.O. Box 350
Hatch, NM 87937
505-267-3226
1-800-292-4454
www.hatch-chile.com

Jane Butel's Cooking School
Pantry
125 Second Street NW
Albuquerque, NM 87102
1-800-472-8229
www.janebutel.com

Jane Butel's Pecos Valley Spice Co.
400 Gold NW, Suite 750
Albuquerque, NM 87102
505-314-0787
1-800-473-TACO (8226)
www.pecosvalley.com

NM Chili.Com
2315 Hendola NE
Albuquerque, NM 87110
505-294-6722
1-888-336-4228
www.nmchili.com
wholesale:
www.wholesalechili.com

Pendery's
1221 Manufacturing Street
Dallas, Texas 75207
1-800-533-1870
www.penderys.com

Santa Fe Chile Co.
500 Sandoval
Santa Fe, NM 87501
505-995-9667
www.chileco.com

Santa Fe School of Cooking
116 West San Francisco Street
Santa Fe, NM 87501
505-983-4511
www.santafeschoolofcooking.com

Velardi's Chile Products
Emily & Roman Velardi
606 Camino Del Pueblo
Bernalillo, NM 87004
505-867-3027

WEST & NORTHWEST

Casa Lucas Market
2934 Twenty-Fourth Street
San Francisco, CA 94110
415-826-4334

La Palma
2884 Twenty-Fourth Street
San Francisco, CA 94110
415-647-1500
fax: 415-647-1710

EAST

The Hot Shoppe
311 S. Clinton St.
Syracuse NY 13202
1-888-468-3287 (HOTEATS)
www.hotshoppe.com

Mo Hotta–Mo Betta
P.O. Box 1026
Savannah, GA 31402
1-800-462-3220
www.mohotta.com

More Great Cookbooks from Clear Light Publishing

FIESTAS FOR FOUR SEASONS
Southwest Entertaining with Jane Butel

By Jane Butel, Photographs by Marcia Keegan

"Full of great menu ideas and recipes featuring Southwest recipes...." **(Wichita Falls *Times Record News*)**

Beautifully illustrated with color photographs, this cookbook presents full menu ideas corresponding to the four seasons as well as an overview of the basics of Southwestern cooking.

ISBN 0940666723
35 color photos,192 pp., 8 x 8 (paperback) $14.95

GOURMET TORTILLAS
Exotic & Traditional Tortilla Dishes

By Karen Howarth

This cookbook shows how to make tortillas flavored and enhanced with a wide variety of surprising additions. It also offers recipes for main dishes from the traditional to the exotic. Great creative fun for all, from kids to gourmet cooks!

ISBN 1574160583
176 pp., 8 x 9¼ (paperback) $14.95

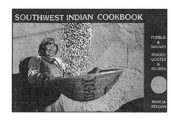

SOUTHWEST INDIAN COOKBOOK
Pueblo & Navajo Images, Quotes & Recipes

Edited and Photographed by Marcia Keegan

"Recipes, striking color photographs and an informative and beguiling text on the food and folklore... [A] loving and poetic presentation of both the cuisines and the people behind them." **(*New York Times*)**

"An amazing mix of history, folklore, photography and recipes from the American Southwest.... An excellent addition to any cook's library." (***New England Review of Books***)

ISBN 0940666030
44 color photos,120 pp., 9 x 6 (paperback) $12.95

Winner of the
R. T. French
Tastemaker
Award

For complete selection of all our titles, visit our web site at
www.clearlightbooks.com

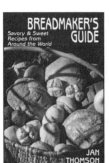

BREADMAKER'S GUIDE
Savory & Sweet Recipes from Around the World

By Jan Thomson

This treasury of instruction, recipes and practical wisdom offers recipes and practical wisdom for every level of expertise, as well as recipes for no-knead yeasted batter bread and alterations for bread machines. An essential addition to the kitchen bookshelf.

ISBN 1574160494
296 pp., 6 x 9 (paperback) $14.95

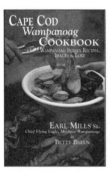

CAPE COD WAMPANOAG COOKBOOK
Traditional New England & Indian Recipes, Images & Lore

By Earl Mills, Sr. & Betty Breen

"*It will make your mouth water!*" (**Midwest Book Review**) Indigenous foods and native lore are the basic ingredients of this cookbook. The recipes, many drawn from favorites from author Earl Mills's Cape Cod restaurant, The Flume, range from chowders to game to seafood to desserts—even a good old-fashioned clambake.

1574160575
Photographs, 296 pp., 6 x 9 (paperback) $14.95

CELEBRATIONS COOKBOOK
Menus Plans, Recipes & Table Decorations

By Myra J. Baucom & Jolynn Baucom-Wright

This unique guide to meal preparation includes a complete menu for each feast and suggestions on dinner table decor. With the help of this mother-daughter team, you can turn any meal into a festive and memorable occasion. Marvelous recipes for every event.

ISBN 1574160621
Illustrations, 8 x 10 (paperback) $14.95

For complete selection of all our titles, visit our web site at www.clearlightbooks.com

CHRISTMAS CELEBRATION
Santa Fe Traditions, Foods & Crafts

By Richard Clawson, Text by Jann Arrington Wolcott

This holiday treasury presents Southwestern recipes, menus, and party plans as well as crafts ideas, decorations, ornaments and gifts. Color illustrations include photographs of festivities and exquisite winter scenes in Santa Fe.

ISBN 0940666685
121 color & 11 B&W photos, 128 pp., 10 x 12 (hardback)
$39.95

CITRUS COOKBOOK
Tantalizing Food & Beverage Recipes from Around the World

By Frank Thomas & Marlene Leopold

This collection of over 200 recipes featuring citrus fruits or flavoring offers everything from variations on standards to mouth-watering originals, including appetizers, salsas, beverages, soups, sauces, dressings, meats, seafood and desserts.

ISBN 1574160567
160 pp., 6 x 9 (paperback) $14.95

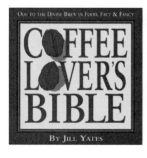

COFFEE LOVER'S BIBLE
Ode to the Divine Brew in Food, Fact & Fancy

By Jill Yates

"All you need to know about coffee and many varieties of hot and cold drinks, plus fantastic desserts." (**Eagle-Tribune Lifestyle**) This enjoyable volume provides 101 recipes for drinks to desserts to savory main dishes as well as all the tips you need from selecting beans to brewing that perfect cup of coffee. With delightful old-style illustrations and quotes.

ISBN 1574160141
Illustrations, 208 pp., 7½ x 7½ (paperback) $12.95

For complete selection of all our titles, visit our web site at www.clearlightbooks.com

COW COUNTRY COOKBOOK

By Dan Cushman,
Drawings by Charlie Russell

"In between the fascinating recipes is a lot of cow-
boy lore. It's a choice little book to savor." (**Come-**
All-Yee) Illustrated by famed Western artist
Charlie Russell, this cookbook contains over 100
pioneer and line camp recipes as well as well as
cowboy anecdotes.

ISBN 0949666189
37 drawings, 176 pp., 9 x 6 (paper) $8.95

HAPPY CAMPER'S COOKBOOK
Eating Well Is Portable™

By Marilyn Abraham & Sandy MacGregor

"A handy cookbook and charming travel guide based on their
experiences living and cooking in a recreational vehicle."
(**Albuquerque Journal**) *"These recipes are quick, simple and fun.*
The advice on everything from grilling to gazpacho is perfect."
(**Jessica Harris, author of The Africa Cookbook**) The easy and
tasty recipes and techniques can be used in the home as well,
especially on the backyard grill.

ISBN 1574160249
125 recipes, 40 Illustrations, 144 pp., 6 x 9 (paperback) $14.95

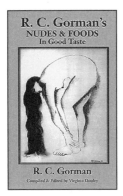

R. C. GORMAN'S NUDES & FOODS
In Good Taste

By R. C. Gorman, Compiled & Edited by Virginia Dooley

"This beautiful cookbook de art is sure to satisfy any artistic
palette.... with 19 chapters of creations from Gorman's own
kitchen and those of relatives, friends and neighbors." (**New**
Mexican)

Filled with anecdotes, culinary delights and works of art that
demonstrate the extraordinary range of Gorman's gifts, *Nudes*
& Foods is a feast for the eye, the palate and the mind.

ISBN 0940666413
55 color plates,142 pp., 8½ x 11 (hardback) $34.95

For complete selection of all our titles, visit our web site at
www.clearlightbooks.com

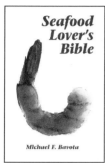

SEAFOOD LOVER'S BIBLE

By Michael F. Bavota

"*Michael F. Bavota knows his seafood....He covers this subject completely in his cookbook, giving 200 recipes that are easy for any home cook to prepare....His chapter on how to buy, handle and cook seafood is very thorough and will be a portion of this cookbook that is as important as the recipes.*" (**Fort Pierce, Fla. Tribune**)

ISBN 1574160273
192 pp., 6 x 9 (paperback) $14.95

SOUPS, STEWS & QUICKBREADS
495 Quick & Easy Recipes from Around the World

By Jan Thomson

"*A cornucopia of imaginative, nutritious, attractive easy gourmet recipes that will delight the eye as they please the palate.*" (***Bookwatch***)

A lifesaver for the busy cook, this book offers hundreds of quick, light and hearty "meals in a bowl" and a nearly endless choice of breads to be served on the side.

ISBN 1574160028
222 pp., 6 x 9 (paperback) $14.95

ORDER FORM

I AM INTERESTED IN PURCHASING THE FOLLOWING TITLES:

TITLE	PRICE	QTY	TOTAL
	SUBTOTAL		
PLEASE ADD: 1st Copy Shipping & Handling $3.50			
Each Additional Copy 50¢			
NM Residents Add 6.6875% Sales Tax			
TOTAL			

SHIP TO:

Name _____ Phone _____

Address _____

City _____ State _____ Zip _____

COMPLETE CATALOG AVAILABLE ON-LINE
www.clearlightbooks.com
or free printed copy, call 1-800-253-2747

ORDER ON-LINE & SAVE
WWW.CLEARLIGHTBOOKS.COM
VISA and MasterCard accepted
Call 1-800-253-2747 for credit card orders

e-mail: service@clearlightbooks.com
823 Don Diego • Santa Fe • New Mexico • 87505
(505) 989-9590 • Fax: (505) 989-9519

This order form may be photocopied & mailed or faxed.